In *Lessons from Eve*, MiChelle Ferguson brilliantly addresses issues that affect every one of us. As I read chapter one, I was amazed at how MiChelle discusses the ways in which insecurities have cost so many people their peace and their provision. I thought, *If I read no further, this chapter alone is worth the entire book.* But as I continued, I discovered that each chapter is filled with insightful truths that would benefit any believer, male or female. There is so much I could say about this book that I could have easily written a foreword for it. But I was asked to write an endorsement, and I wholeheartedly endorse this amazing book, and I thank MiChelle for her willingness to write it. It is simply powerful and so needed!

RICK RENNER
Author, Bible teacher, and broadcaster

Pastor MiChelle's book gives a very interesting look at how Satan was successful with the first woman, Eve, causing her to abandon her rightful place in God's blessings for her. In addition, Pastor MiChelle's personal testimony not only will greatly assist many women in their struggles but also aid many men who also are affected by the same challenges. Reading this book will assist everyone in defeating Satan's plans to destroy them and instead cause the reader to walk in victory in this life.

BISHOP KEITH A. BUTLER

You will be tremendously blessed as you read my friend MiChelle's new book! Through her own life experiences and God's Word, she teaches you how to overcome and walk in victory! Get ready, you are about to go to a higher level!

KATE MCVEIGH
Teacher and author of *The Blessing of Favor* and *Get Over It*

Lessons from Eve humanizes Eve in a way we've never experienced. MiChelle Ferguson pulls the reader in with fresh revelation from Heaven to transform the heart and mind. A must-read for women of all ages!

HEATHER LINDSEY

Lessons from Eve is a powerful and thought-provoking exploration through God's Word. It explores the themes of temptation, sin, and consequences in a way that is relatable, applicable, and riveting. Michelle expertly weaves together the biblical text with her own interpretation, creating a rich and engaging narrative that will leave readers contemplating the lessons of Eve's story, and how it applies to us, long after you've finished reading this incredible book.

TIM TIMBERLAKE
Senior pastor of Celebration Church
Author of the bestselling book *The Power of 1440*

MiChelle did an outstanding job in sharing information that can increase our lives. Take full advantage of the nuggets shared in this life changing book. Through understanding and application, I'm confident that the tools shared will give you the answers you've been praying for. The life of Eve is such a powerful teaching that has endless lessons we can all learn from, like "Knowing Who You Are," to "Looks Can Be Deceiving," and "Using Your Influence Wisely," just to name a few. The twelve chapters in this book cover twelve different lessons that will assist us in growing and developing into the women God predestined us to be. So, get ready as you embark upon a deep dive into each of these chapters because transformation is yours!

DR. DEEDEE FREEMAN
First Lady of Spirit of Faith Christian Center

OVERCOME SELF-SABOTAGE, TAKE CONTROL OF
YOUR LIFE, AND KEEP YOUR CROWN

LESSONS
FROM
Eve

MICHELLE FERGUSON

Published by Harrison House Publishers
Shippensburg, PA 17257

ISBN 13 TP: 978-1-6675-0231-1
ISBN 13 eBook: 978-1-6675-0232-8

For Worldwide Distribution, Printed in the U.S.A.
1 2 3 4 5 6 7 8 / 27 26 25 24 23

Contents

Foreword

I was totally mesmerized, weak-kneed jelly, gazing into those deep blue eyes. Ah!

My first marriage was falling apart. I really *believed* him when he said how sorry he was and swore he'd never hit me again. Or at least, I wanted to believe him.

Promises were broken. Bank accounts drained. I tried to hold it all together by myself. I excused bad behavior and supported him through every treatment program and relapse like a loyal wife.

When his addiction spiraled completely out of control and he threatened the safety of my son, when his violence left us bruised and terrified, when even the law couldn't protect us, I finally had to put my trust in the Lord.

It was about time.

I'd like to think that my confidence had been in God the whole time. But now I realize I willingly surrendered my position, my power, and my purpose, and handed it all straight over to the enemy.

Oh, but those blue eyes! *Dang!*

Looks can be *so* deceiving, can't they? Those sincere tears and heartfelt apologies. Promises. More promises. Deep down, I knew I'd been deceived and fallen for a *big lie* hook, line, and sinker! I think that's what hurt the most. My life wasn't stolen. I gave it away. Sucker!

"Sorry, Eve. I think I owe you an apology. I've totally misjudged you, girl!"

In *Lessons from Eve*, author MiChelle Ferguson raises an uncomfortable but critical question: "Are we *still* falling for some of the same old traps that Eve did?"

Who, *us?*

We're probably a lot more like Eve than we want to believe. The enemy would love nothing more than to disrupt the peace in our own little corner of paradise. Steal our joy. Stir up doubt in our hearts and talk us into giving up our God-given authority without firing a single shot!

Words—mere words.

Never underestimate the power of suggestion. Don't even entertain the serpent. Stop listening to all the wrong people, because whoever has your ear controls your life!

My friend MiChelle is a fierce, face-forward, put-your-money-where-your-mouth-is, go-big-or-go-home kind of girl! She's someone who loves the Lord with all her heart—enough to take Him at His Word no matter what the circumstances look like.

There are a lot of people who teach on faith from a life that has never stepped out or stepped up into anything bigger than themselves. Not this girl! She's the real deal! She has fought and won the big faith battles in her life and never given in!

Her book is full of fresh and usable revelation. Don't be fooled by the lies of this world! She'll teach you how to guard your heart and protect your identity in Christ. Be confident in who you are and what God has called you to do. In other words, you've got it going on, and the devil just hates it!

In her moment of weakness, Eve bought the lie of the enemy, willingly gave away her authority, and created her own demise. Oh, Eve!

Well, *not* us! *Not today,* devil! We're wise to your tricks now! We've learned our *Lessons from Eve.*

Blessings!

NICOLE CRANK
Host of *The Nicole Crank Show*
USA Today bestselling author and speaker
Senior co-pastor of FaithChurch.com

The Fall of a Queen

Genesis 3

Now the serpent was more subtil than any beast of the field which the Lord God had made. And he said unto the woman, Yea, hath God said, Ye shall not eat of every tree of the garden? And the woman said unto the serpent, We may eat of the fruit of the trees of the garden: But of the fruit of the tree which is in the midst of the garden, God hath said, Ye shall not eat of it, neither shall ye touch it, lest ye die. And the serpent said unto the woman, Ye shall not surely die: For God doth know that in the day ye eat thereof, then your eyes shall be opened, and ye shall be as gods, knowing good and evil. And when the woman saw that the tree was good for food, and that it was pleasant to the eyes, and a tree to be desired to make one wise, she took of the fruit thereof, and did eat, and gave also unto her husband with her; and he did eat.

And the eyes of them both were opened, and they knew that they were naked; and they sewed fig leaves together, and made themselves aprons. And they heard the voice of the Lord God walking in the garden in the cool of the day: and Adam and his wife hid themselves from the presence of the Lord God amongst the trees of the garden. And the Lord God called unto Adam, and said unto him, Where art thou? And he said, I heard thy voice in the garden, and I was afraid, because I was naked; and I hid myself. And he said, Who told thee that thou wast naked? Hast thou eaten of the tree, whereof I commanded thee that thou shouldest not eat? And the man said, The woman whom thou gavest to be with me, she gave me of the tree, and I did eat.

And the Lord God said unto the woman, What is this that thou hast done? And the woman said, The serpent beguiled me, and I did eat. And the Lord God said unto the serpent, Because thou hast done this, thou art cursed above all cattle, and above every beast of the field; upon thy belly shalt thou go, and dust shalt thou eat all the days of thy life: And I will put enmity between thee and the woman, and between thy seed and her seed; it shall bruise thy head, and thou shalt bruise his heel. Unto the woman he said, I will greatly multiply thy sorrow and thy conception; in sorrow thou shalt bring forth children; and thy desire shall be to thy husband, and he shall rule over thee.

And unto Adam he said, Because thou hast hearkened unto the voice of thy wife, and hast eaten of the tree, of which I commanded thee, saying, Thou shalt not eat of it: cursed is the ground for thy sake; in sorrow shalt thou eat of it all the days of thy life; Thorns also and thistles shall it bring forth to thee; and thou shalt eat the herb of the field; In the sweat of thy face shalt thou eat bread, till thou return unto the ground; for out of it wast thou taken: for dust thou art, and unto dust shalt thou return. And Adam called his wife's name Eve; because she was the mother of all living. Unto Adam also and to his wife did the Lord God make coats of skins, and clothed them.

And the Lord God said, Behold, the man is become as one of us, to know good and evil: and now, lest he put forth his hand, and take also of the tree of life, and eat, and live for ever: Therefore the Lord God sent him forth from the garden of Eden, to till the ground from whence he was taken. So he drove out the man; and he placed at the east of the garden of Eden Cherubims, and a flaming sword which turned every way, to keep the way of the tree of life.

Introduction

I often like to think about what I will do when I get to Heaven. I imagine myself in the throne room of God, singing with the angels, worshiping the Father with love and gratitude, and thanking Jesus for making it possible for me to be there. I see myself embracing my loved ones who have gone on before me. I especially look forward to meeting the three babies that I lost on the way to becoming a mom. They'll probably be all grown up and will show me around the place. I don't know if dogs go to Heaven or not, but if they do, I also have some canines I will be looking for, particularly my little papillon, Dylan. I also think about how cool it will be to converse with some of my favorite Bible heroes, like Esther, Elijah, Abraham, Mary, and the apostle Paul.

I love to think about the custom mansion that Jesus has prepared for me—what it looks like, what style it will be fashioned in. I change my mind so much about what I like, but God knows what I like better than I do, so it will be a real surprise to see what He designs for me. What an exciting time it will be to walk the streets of gold; run through the pearly gates; hear the heavenly instruments; and behold the landscapes, colors, streams, and rivers that are sure to be much more vibrant and radiant than anything I have seen or experienced on earth. Oh—and let's not forget the glorious body that awaits me in Heaven. I can see myself saying, "Ummm, where's the mirror?" In fact, I'm pretty sure if my mansion isn't equipped with floor-to-ceiling mirrors, I'll promptly request them.

There's one more thing I can see myself doing upon my arrival in Heaven—asking for Eve's address so I can pay her a visit. I admit this request isn't quite so glorious or joyous, and if I am honest, it's not quite fitting for such a holy place. But on so many occasions I have thought, *How could you, Eve?!?!*

HOW COULD YOU, EVE?

I am sure I am not the only woman who has some serious questions for the first woman. Like—how did you blow it so badly when you *woke up* with a man? She didn't have to wonder about being found or wonder when her man was coming. The moment she opened her eyes, he was there, and I know for a fact that Adam was fine! How do I know that? Well, there was no one else to compare him to! There was no wishing that he was taller, thinner, lighter, darker or more muscular. He was the one and only standard.

The same goes for Eve. We know she woke up with a body with the perfect dimensions, because there was nobody to compare her to. No supermodels or gorgeous actresses were strutting around causing Eve to think, *Man, I wish I looked like that!* She was the standard! Eve didn't need to check to see if Adam noticed another beautiful woman walking by using that bionic, supernatural vision we ladies have to see if our man has noticed some other female. Eve had *none of that!* She was literally the most beautiful woman Adam had ever seen.

Let's not forget, not only did she have a man, but he also had his own home that was paid for and given to him by God. I've been blessed to behold some gorgeous landscapes in my life and travels, but I am sure none of them compare to the beauty of the garden of Eden. Also, Adam had multiple jobs, and he had power! You know we ladies can appreciate a man with power. This man was dressing and keeping that garden with dominion and authority. All the creatures of the earth were subject to him, and he was naming them.

I can just see Eve being like, "Hey, boo, what do you want to call this beautiful orange animal with black stripes?"

Adam thinks and responds, "Hmmmm, tiger, baby. I'm going to call him a tiger."

Eve probably got chills, like, "Alright, baby, I like that! Tiger it is!"

Let's keep it real. It had to be so attractive watching him take authority and handle his business. Clearly, Adam had it going on, but that wasn't even the best part. Let me submit this to all of the single women reading this book: The sexiest thing about a man is not his six pack or lack thereof. It's not the size of his bank account or the type of car he drives or how large his house is.

The sexiest thing about a man is his relationship with God. All of those other things can fade away in an instant, but a man with a strong relationship with God can survive any storm and come out on top with God on his side. That man can speak to mountains, and they move. That man can walk in restoration even after the biggest disappointments. That man can have confidence and peace even in the valley of the shadow of death. That man can speak life to dead situations and healing into diseased circumstances.

God Himself used to come down and commune with Adam in the cool of the day! Let's please not make light of the fact that this man had this relationship with God *before* Eve came along. Eve was not missionary dating, hoping to get Adam saved or more committed to the things of God. No, this man was telling her what the Lord was saying! Wow—what a man! Seriously, Eve, with that kind of setup, *how could you?*

MIRROR, MIRROR ON THE WALL

I remember, a few years back, when dealing with some uncomfortable female issues, blurting out sarcastically, "Thanks, EVE!" If she had just kept it tight, things would be so much better. I held on to that attitude concerning her for a while, until one day I sensed the Lord say to me, "You do the same things that you criticize Eve for." That was not easy to hear. I thought for sure that had to be the devil talking. *Let me cast that out right now! There is no way God could be saying that to me because, after all, I would never be that gullible or foolish, right?* But as I took a deeper look into Eve's story, I realized how true God's statement was. I felt compelled to stop judging Eve and to take a long, hard look in the mirror. *Am I falling for the same traps she did? Am I making the same mistakes?* The truth is, if we're honest, we can all see a bit of ourselves in Eve.

We have a place we belong, a purpose we've received from God, and the peace and tranquility that come from being in God's will. I like to call that place our own personal garden of Eden. Nothing compares to it. There we receive power in purpose and the grace to run the race set before us. But like Eve, many times we get kicked out of our own gardens by falling for the same tricks and traps that Satan, through the serpent, used to get Eve to forfeit her God-given place in this world. A key word in Genesis 3:1 describes how Satan dethroned a queen—*subtil* (in the KJV) or *subtle* (in our modern English). *Subtle* speaks volumes to me because it reveals a powerful truth we cannot ignore: Satan was not powerful enough to strip Eve of her God-given glory, but he was crafty enough to deceive her into laying it down herself.

SAME PLAN, DIFFERENT DAY

Here we are, thousands of years later, and Satan is still using the same tactics with you and me. The Bible warns us not to be ignorant of Satan's devices (see 2 Cor. 2:11). The thief doesn't come for an empty house. Despite how you may feel about your life, the truth is, you've got it going on just like Adam and Eve did. God sent His Son, Jesus, to save and redeem you because *you matter!* If you were the only person here on earth, Jesus still would have come just for you. You are important, and this world needs you. Don't be fooled into forfeiting your own place of victory. We have an advantage, because we have the blood of Jesus and the revelation of the Word of God to help us walk in total fulfillment and grace.

We don't read the story of Adam and Eve so we can sit back, wag our fingers, and shake our heads in disgust. Instead, it's a treasure trove of wisdom and revelation we can apply. If we pay attention, it can help us walk out the plans and purposes God has for our lives. Satan has no new tricks. The Bible says to "Be sober, be vigilant; because your adversary the devil walks about like a roaring lion, seeking whom he may devour" (1 Pet. 5:8 NKJV). I don't know about you, but I am tired of watching him devour lives, relationships, self-esteems, purposes, and callings. It's time for us to come off of that menu.

I am so thankful the Lord compelled me to take a deeper look into the fall of beautiful Eve. I now realize that this story is a gift to us all, but especially to women, a master class of all master classes. Although the enemy continues to attempt to quietly deceive, we can learn from Mother Eve how to shut those subtle doors in our own lives so that we not only stay in our own gardens of Eden but thrive there.

Okay, Eve. I'm listening, and I'm ready.

Lesson One

Know Who You Are

But of the fruit of the tree which is in the midst of the garden, God hath said, Ye shall not eat of it, neither shall ye touch it, lest ye die. And the serpent said unto the woman, Ye shall not surely die: For God doth know that in the day ye eat thereof, then your eyes shall be opened, and ye shall be as gods, knowing good and evil (Genesis 3:3–5).

With my newfound perspective concerning Eve— meaning, I forfeited my plans to jump her in Heaven—I found myself searching for a deeper understanding of what actually happened in the garden. What was it about the serpent that was more attractive than what Eve had been given? What was she hoping to gain? What did she feel like she was missing? And most importantly, what can

I learn from her mistakes? We all know Eve experienced a pretty big failure that just about cost her everything, but I wonder—How many of us are unknowingly following in her footsteps?

DYING TO BECOME WHAT YOU ALREADY ARE

In my first year of Bible college, I found myself at a crossroads. I was happy to be there, and I was learning so much. I had been blessed with good friends, great instructors, and a fully furnished apartment on campus. For the first time in my life, I felt like I was in the perfect will of God, yet something still felt very wrong. I had finally discovered my God-given purpose, and I was pursuing it. But as I lay in a doctor's office in Broken Arrow, Oklahoma, I realized that something was still missing.

It was almost a full-circle moment for me. The doctor looked at my face and said, "I know you." My parents had always told me that (even though I was in my 20s) my face still looked the same as when I was born. I always thought they were exaggerating until the doctor continued, "I remember your face. I delivered you over 20 years ago." I had indeed been born in Tulsa, just a few miles away, when my parents were in Bible school themselves. The doctor went on to recall my parents' names and some very cool details of my birth.

I tried to smile and (frankly) care as he was reminiscing, but I could barely appreciate the irony of the moment because of the reason for my visit to his office. I had never felt so ill in my life, but I didn't know what was wrong, and I wondered, *How can this be happening?* I had just made a major change for the better in my life—switching from the university I had been attending to a Bible school so that I could answer God's call on my life. I had finished one semester, but I wasn't sure if, physically, I'd be able to finish the next.

It was early 1998, almost one full year after the heart-breaking tragedy that had inspired me to take the leap of faith and enroll in Bible school. Growing up, I knew a few people who really impacted me. One of them was our church Music Minister, Geoffrey Davis, Sr. A man of great talent and charisma, he had chosen to give his gifts back to the Lord, and as a result, he had blessed so many lives.

Then, on Thursday, January 9, 1997, I got a call that changed my life. I had just finished my classes for the day at the prestigious University of Michigan, and I was sitting on my futon in my tiny dorm room located on South State Street in Ann Arbor, Michigan, when the phone rang. There had been a plane crash, and there were no survivors. I took a deep breath, dreading the next sentence that was sure to come. I didn't know who was on the plane, but I knew by the tone of the voice on the phone that it was someone I loved. It was as if time slowed down to a crawl. I could almost count each breath of the caller as she uttered the words, "Brother Geoff was on the plane."

The next few days were a blur. As I spent time with family and friends, I just couldn't wrap my head around the reality that such a horrible thing could happen to such a wonderful person. It brought new meaning to a familiar phrase that I had often ignored: Life is short, so make the most of it. I remember sitting in a room with Brother Geoff's two young sons and watching his seven-year-old play his little synthesizer with the same gifts and talents that his dad had blessed the world with. It was almost too much to bear.

After several days, we all gathered, not for a funeral, but for a celebration of his life. The service could have been filled with sadness and grief, but it was anything but that. As I sat through the phenomenal memorial filled with songs that Brother Geoff had written and stories and testimonies of the lives he had touched, I decided that I wanted to make an impact as great as he had with whatever time I had left.

A few nights later, when I returned to my dorm room, I knelt before the Lord and asked Him to show me my purpose. I asked Him to use my life to make a mark that would last, and that's when I received my call to the ministry. My plans had changed. What I had been doing was good, but I knew God had something so much better for me. So I packed my bags, left my university, and moved across the country to enroll in Bible school. Brother Geoff had impacted my life in so many ways, but none greater than this. Even as I write this today, 25 years later, I realize that God took a horrible situation and used it for good in my life, and I am forever grateful.

A year after Brother Geoff's death, I was right where I was supposed to be—in training for the ministry and excited about the call of God on my life. Except I was stuck on a medical bed awaiting a diagnosis. I felt like I was dying right in the midst of my newfound purpose. What was wrong? I had worn my body down so much that, even though I had received this great opportunity, it was stifled by the choices I had made.

You see, I grew up in a very attractive family. They are all thin, fit, and trim, but for as long as I can remember, I was the plump oddball out. I was the chubby girl. I remember, at the age of eight, watching my friends in the school cafeteria eat their lunches filled with sandwiches, chips, fruit roll-ups, and juice boxes while I waited for my microwavable weight-loss meal to be heated up and brought to me along with a bottle of water. *Why was I born this way? Why can't I eat like the other kids? Why can't I drink juice like everyone else?* I internalized my feelings and wished upon every star that I could have a different body. After all, something was wrong with me, and I was so aware of it.

Although I can recall many wonderful memories from my childhood, none stick out to me more than the fat jokes, rejection, and numerous diet failures that I experienced as a result of being an overweight child. I despised myself. That mentality followed me all throughout my adolescent years and into early adulthood. It impacted every decision I made. I just wasn't enough. Actually, I was literally too much of all the wrong things. Looking back, I don't know why I did not realize that defeatist attitude would follow me into my purposed place.

I had met some other girls at Bible school who were also desperate to lose weight at any cost. We talked and cried and bonded over just how empty we felt and how everything would be so much better if we were thin. It got so bad that we developed a slogan that we used to keep us inspired in our extreme and unhealthy attempts at weight-loss: "BETTER DEAD THAN FAT!"

I had succumbed to disordered patterns and thinking while believing I was doing the right thing because, after all, I felt like I was nothing. For months, I had engaged in foolish and dangerous practices that were detrimental to my health. And now, it was payday. My body was weak, and I had developed a condition that cut my first year short and sent me right back home and right out of my recently celebrated purpose. Thankfully, my Bible school sent my course work home with me so that I could complete the year with my peers. That experience made clear to me what had been missing. It wasn't my weight that needed to change, but how I saw myself.

It seems that Eve found herself in a situation like mine... *dying to become what she already was*. After all, I just wanted to be loved and accepted. I longed to be chosen and important. I needed to be noticed and admired. But like Eve, I hadn't realized that I had already attained all of that love and attention from the Creator of the universe. I needed to recognize the importance of what I already had and who I already was in Him. Sure, I could take better care of my body, but the strength to accomplish that wasn't found in denying my value; instead, agreeing with how God saw me released the grace that I so desperately needed. Just like us, Eve was fearfully and wonderfully made, but she clearly didn't have full ownership of that revelation.

Otherwise, she would not have been so easily lured into looking for it somewhere else.

The bait Satan used to hook Eve was closely connected to her identity. In the serpent's initial approach to her in Genesis 3:5, he not only insinuated that God was lying to her, but he also said God's real reason for limiting her from that tree was to keep her down. I imagine she felt that as a direct challenge to her worth. No wonder she fell for it. How many times have we ladies made messes in our own lives because we felt someone else didn't recognize or appreciate our splendor? But that wasn't the truth of the matter in the garden of Eden. God did introduce a boundary into Adam and Eve's lives, but not to devalue or lessen who they were; He did it to protect them.

I think about the serpent's line, "You will be as gods knowing good and evil" (Genesis 3:5), and I wonder what about that was so appealing. Adam and Eve were already made in the god-class. God made them in His image and likeness. And He gave them dominion and authority over all living things on the earth, including all of the creatures and plants (see Gen. 1:26–30). In other words, they already were the "gods" of their world. Satan was offering Eve something she already had. Because she wasn't secure in that fact, she traded her glory in an attempt to attain something she already had. Her insecurity not only cost Eve her livelihood, but it also hindered her ability to see God's boundary as a demonstration of His love and the value He placed on her. More about that a little later.

IDENTITY CRISIS

Insecurities have cost a great many people their peace and provision. If left unchecked, insecurity will steal your focus and limit your effectiveness. Satan is after your identity, and if you don't know your value, you are sure to forfeit it for a counterfeit just as Eve did. If the enemy can crack your identity, then he can crack your life. The enemy has effectively used this tool for thousands of years against humankind.

As a teen and young adult, I bought the lie that I was only valuable if I was at my goal weight. If I was over that number, it didn't matter to me if I was killing myself to get there. This was the enemy's way of getting me to eliminate myself. So many of us have fallen into this trap of compromised relationships, purposes, standards, and dreams by believing the lies of the wicked one. So many are lost and searching in all the wrong places for what can only be found in Christ Jesus. And Satan uses that insecurity against them.

In the New Testament, Satan even tried to run this same scheme on Jesus several times. In Matthew 4, Jesus had been fasting for 40 days. Then, like an old broken record, we see Satan challenging Jesus' identity in an attempt to trap Him. "And when the tempter [Satan] came to him [Jesus], he said, If thou be the Son of God, command that these stones be made bread" (Matt. 4:3). But Jesus wasn't fooled. He answered, "It is written, Man shall not live by bread alone, but by every word that proceedeth out of the mouth of God" (Matt. 4:4). Satan then took Jesus to the top of the temple in Jerusalem and said, "If thou be the Son of God, cast thyself down: for it is written, He shall give his angels charge over thee: and in their hands they shall bear thee up, lest at any time thou dash thy foot against a stone" (Matt. 4:6). But once again, Jesus answered him with Scripture: "It is written again, Thou shalt not temtp the Lord thy God" (Matt. 4:7).

Satan began his temptation with, "If thou be the Son of God." Jesus' hunger after fasting had nothing to do with whether or not He was the Son of God. Clearly, Satan was looking for a weakness—the same one he often finds in you and me. What if Jesus hadn't been solid on who He was? What if insecurities had distracted Him from His mission, causing Him to try to prove something to someone or something that did not matter? Thank God we will never know the answer to that question. Jesus knew who He was even in the face of a direct challenge. I love how Jesus so clearly stated the truth of the matter: "Thou shalt not tempt the Lord thy God." That *"thy God"* is powerful, as if to say, "Not only am I the Son of God, but I am your God too, whether you want to recognize it or not." Jesus did not let the questions and temptations from outside forces, like the enemy, rattle or compromise the inward confidence He had in His value, purpose, and focus.

We see this demonstrated again in Matthew 27, when Jesus walked out His greatest act of love on the cross. As Jesus hung on the cross, the people who walked by reviled Him, saying, "Thou that destroyest the temple, and buildest it in three days, save thyself. If thou be the Son of God, come down from the cross" (Matt. 27:40). The spiritual leaders of Israel—the chief priests, scribes, and elders—also mocked Him, saying, "He saved others; himself he cannot save. If he be the King of Israel, let him now come down from the cross, and we will believe him" (Matt. 27:42).

Once again, the enemy was working hard to find a crack in Jesus' identity. "If You really are who You say You are, then prove it! If You want us to really believe You, then do that! I thought You were all that, but look at You now! Hahaha!" Undoubtedly, most of us have dealt with or felt these things within the struggles of our own lives. I've served in full-time ministry for over two decades now, and I've learned that the number one issue when dealing with women struggling with self-harming practices (promiscuity, cutting, eating disorders, and so forth) is identity. To help them walk into their freedom, I must first strengthen their understanding of their identity and value in Christ. The better they feel about themselves, the better the decisions they tend to make *concerning* themselves. In essence, you will never protect what you don't value.

This is the miracle that Christ afforded us with His death, burial, and resurrection. He gave us back the identity and value that Adam and Eve forfeited in the garden thousands of years ago. You are not damaged goods; you are a masterpiece! That is the type of confidence that Jesus died to give you. Think about what love He showed upon that cross, what pain He endured to erase the past and give us a new life.

God made us brilliantly in His own image and likeness. Life may cause us to question or challenge that, but we can rest in Him, knowing that even before we could love Him, He loved us enough to secure us with His blood. If God

Himself, who knows and sees all things, counts us as valuable, who are we to question His opinion? Who are we to listen to anyone or anything that contradicts His truth?

LIMITING BELIEFS

Your beliefs about yourself have a direct connection to the peace and success you will experience in your life. God has graciously blessed each one of us with our own individual gifts and talents. However, many people don't experience the fullness of what God has provided. It's easy to blame the trials and tribulations we've faced or past events in our lives as reasons why we are living limited and unfulfilled lives, but the true cause is found in our own inward views. We see this clearly demonstrated in the lives of the children of Israel. God had brought them to their place of destiny through many trials and tribulations. They had experienced God's miraculous power throughout their journey from Egypt to the Promised Land. However, at every challenge, their confidence faltered despite God's promises and the faithfulness He consistently demonstrated to them. As a result, they lost out on their future.

> *And they told him, and said, We came unto the land whither thou sentest us, and surely it floweth with milk and honey; and this is the fruit of it. Nevertheless the people be strong that dwell in the land, and the cities are walled, and very great: and moreover, we saw the children of Anak there. The Amalekites dwell in the land of the south: and the Hittites, and the Jebusites, and the Amorites,*

dwell in the mountains: and the Canaanites dwell by the sea, and by the coast of Jordan. And Caleb stilled the people before Moses, and said, Let us go up at once, and possess it; for we are well able to overcome it. But the men that went up with him said, We be not able to go up against the people; for they are stronger than we (Numbers 13:27–31).

The Promised Land was exactly as God had promised, flowing with milk and honey. God had proven time and time again that He was with them and that He valued them. However, verse 31 reveals their beliefs about themselves. They had not yet fought a battle, yet they had already called themselves defeated. Their defeat wasn't at the hands of their enemies but at the hands of their own limiting beliefs about themselves. Caleb was right when he said they were well able to overcome anyone and anything in their way, but his outside voice could not still their inward insecurities. In response to Caleb's assertions, they argued, "And there we saw the giants, the sons of Anak, which come of the giants: and we were in our own sight as grasshoppers, and so we were in their sight" (Num. 13:33). The problem was how they saw themselves—as already defeated grasshoppers.

This generation of the children of Israel did not get to experience their Promised Land but instead died in the wilderness because of their own grasshopper mentality (see Num. 14:30–31). The irony in this story is like many of our own stories. God saw them as champions and giant slayers, but they saw themselves as squashable bugs. As a result, their lives reflected the latter. What a revelation. We play a part in our own victories. God can bring you to victory, but it's up to you to do what's necessary to obtain it.

This revelation helped me overcome the self-sabotaging behavior that eventually cut my first year of Bible school short. Once I arrived home, my diagnosis required that I be kept in an isolated room because my immune system had been compromised. I wasn't allowed to venture out of my room or even the house for weeks. Any visitors who came to see me had to wear protective gear like mask and gloves in order to limit the number of germs I was exposed to. The days felt long, and the nights were lonely and agonizing, but as I look back these many years later, I thank God for those days. In that silence, the Lord was able to speak to me concerning my limiting beliefs about myself. He reminded me of a very painful day when I had allowed the word *almost* to be written on my heart.

I had been hanging out with a good friend of mine at Bible school. He was an anointed man of God with a call on his life and also a star basketball player. I truly enjoyed his company, but we were nothing more than platonic friends. In fact, I was trying to match him with a friend of mine. But for some reason, we started talking about my prospects for marriage. He first complimented me on my personality and expressed how cool of a girl he thought I was. Perhaps he was trying to soften the blow that he was about to deliver. My heart sank as he then explained to me that I *almost* had the whole package and was *almost* marriage material. I fought back tears as he explained that I would have been every man's dream girl if I just had a better body. I was *almost* enough for someone to love me, but just a little too tall and a little too big. *Ouch!* I wish I could say that I checked him right there on the spot, but instead, I just thanked him for the compliment and kept it moving. It hurt, but the saddest part of the story is that I believed him. I believed his thoughts about me more than I did God's.

As I lay in my room recalling this horrible experience, the Lord showed me that if I wanted to thrive in my life, I had to change who I was going to believe. Unfortunately, my friend wasn't the first person to say such horrible things to me or about me. But those opinions were contrary to God's thoughts about me. I was exhausted from trying to live up to other people's standards and expectations. I decided that enough was enough, and I began focusing on scriptures that directly spoke to my value. I pondered them repeatedly. I read them out loud over and over again. I knew I needed to rewrite the narrative in my mind, so I kept at it.

One of my favorite passages was, "But you are a chosen people, a royal priesthood, a holy nation, God's special possession, that you may declare the praises of him who called you out of darkness into his wonderful light" (1 Pet. 2:9 NIV). To be *chosen* means other options were available. I could feel the chains of rejection and depression breaking off of me as I uttered, "The God of the universe chose me. He loves me, and there's not a thing I could do to make Him love me more! He loves me completely just as I am!" The more I meditated on these truths, the stronger I became, and eventually I began to love myself.

After a few months of recovery, I was able to return to school. I graduated with honors and entered full-time ministry. About all of that *almost* stuff—it turns out my friend was wrong. Several years later, a wonderful man proposed to me, and I married him in a gorgeous wedding dress. I am convinced that if I had not challenged those limiting beliefs about what I could have, I would have missed out on the wonderful life I have today, and you probably would not be reading this book.

So much more exists for you on the other side of rejection and disappointment. It starts with recognizing God's great love for you and the value He places on you. Never let your value be determined by other people's preferences. If they did not create you or die on the cross for you, then don't give them the power to override what God has already said about you. You are His chosen, and you are His masterpiece. With Him, you can overcome any challenge that gets in your way.

Know What You Are Working With

And the Lord God said, It is not good that the man should be alone; I will make him an help meet for him (Genesis 2:18).

It was not a coincidence that Satan chose Eve to be the door he used to enact the fall of humankind. I've often pondered the why behind this choice. *Why did Satan go after Eve? Was it that she was weak? Or did he see her as especially powerful?* The more I have studied the Word of God on this subject, the more I've come to realize how mighty women really are. It's frustrating to think that Satan seems to have a greater understanding of that than we do, making it easier for him to deceive smart and capable women, just like he did Eve.

THE BEAUTY OF A WOMAN

To increase our revelation on the beauty of women, we must start from the beginning with God's purpose for creating women. Genesis 2:18 clearly speaks to the origin of women. God had already created the earth, the waters, the fields, the animals, the garden, and the man. Because I can imagine the brilliance of everything He had created, I found myself pondering this statement, "It is not good for the man to be alone." I looked up that word for *good* in the original Hebrew and found that it means "beautiful, best, bountiful, cheerful, and at ease." So God was saying—despite all the wonder He had already created, it was not beautiful, best, bountiful, or cheerful for the man to remain alone. Clearly, Adam's life would not be at ease the way God intended it to be if he continued in that state. *Wow.* That sounds like quite an issue that God had to solve simply because His abundant love for man demanded the best.

To adequately resolve this situation, God needed to do it in His nature! Whatever any of us do or don't do is done according to our nature, whether good or bad. For instance, chronically late people are late because that's part of their nature. I have some people in my life who will not arrive on time to an event of mine unless I tell them it starts thirty minutes earlier than it does. I do this because I know they will approach my event in their nature—which is to be late. God is no different! Everything He does is according to His nature, including addressing this *not good* situation with His first man.

It's ironic that we, as women, tend to feel like we are not enough when, in fact, we were created according to the very nature of the almighty God, who is not just enough. He is El Shaddai, the God of *more* than enough! We were God's answer to a not good situation. In fact, once God made the woman, God beheld His creation and finally said it was *very good* (see Gen. 1:31). Did you see that? We were created to take *not good* and make it *very good!* That is the true beauty of women.

It's no wonder the enemy invests so much time and energy into devaluing women. When I lived in Dallas, Texas, I daily drove down a particular freeway on my way to work that people often referred to as the "red light district." Every day, I felt disgusted seeing horrible billboards splashed with half-naked women in suggestive poses. I often thought, *Is this all we are worth?* Why do we rarely see men being exploited on billboards, in movies, or in music videos? Why do men get a pass for extra pounds, wrinkles, or bald heads, while women are discounted for it? Make no mistake about it, Satan develops his tactics with purpose.

God had empowered Eve to transition the *not good* into *very good*. But she didn't know Satan could reverse that power and use her to take the *very good* back to *not good*. That was never God's intention for women, yet the enemy is desperate to pervert the phenomenal gift God built into women by strategically exploiting and tearing down the fabric and worth of a woman. You are not defined by the texture of your hair or the size of your body parts. You are more than just the color of your skin, the curves of your hips, and the stature of your frame. You are a queen who was created and equipped by almighty God! You are endowed with power from above. This world tries to define beauty by the outside appearance only, but don't be fooled into selling yourself short. Your outward beauty is merely a celebration of the inward majesty given to you by God.

THE HELP?

In Genesis 2:18, when God said, "It is not good for the man to be alone," His solution to the problem was, "I will make him an help meet for him." Often, we get caught up on that word *help*. It is easy to read that word *helper* in a way that implies second-class citizenship. In actuality, the word *help* defines function, not worth. The more I understood this, the easier it was to identify yet another plot the enemy uses against women. If he can get us to reject our place as helpers, then he can succeed in cutting off the benefits associated with that role. As women, we must recognize that it is not an insult but an honor to be called a *help meet*.

This is true for several reasons. First, as helpers we are automatically thrust into the class of the Holy Spirit, who is the supreme Helper. When Jesus ascended to Heaven after His resurrection, He said it was better that He leave so that the Holy Spirit could come. That is a powerful statement that speaks to the gift that is the divine Helper. What a blessing it is to be in His class.

Second, being made as those who are called to help affords us an amazing set of skills. God will not call us do to something without equipping us with all we need to get the job done. For example, let's consider a painter and his helper. The painter must have the grace to complete the task of painting while the helper may be called on to do a greater variety of tasks, like painting, cleaning, organizing, scheduling, and whatever else is required to help the painter accomplish the goal. That means the helper needs to have multiple skills to truly be effective.

Likewise, when a woman is walking in her purpose as a helper, she has access to the entire pool of the grace and the anointing of the heavenly Father. God opened the full catalog of His power to women to equip us to get the job done. It is no coincidence that women tend to be great multitaskers and can juggle many responsibilities and tasks all at the same time. That's not by happenstance; that is by His marvelous design. So let me say this clearly: Don't let negative challenges, situations, or circumstances get you down. Whatever comes your way, you have all that you need to overcome it available to you through Christ. Make no mistake about it, you were created to be a very powerful woman.

Now it makes a lot more sense to me why Satan would aim to shut Eve down. With all she was created to be, all she was empowered to do, she was truly a force to be reckoned with—just like you and me. I am convinced, if Eve had recognized all she was working with, she would have made a better decision. It all comes down to what you know. Although Satan tries, you don't have to forfeit your crown and succumb to his destructive plans.

WOMEN OF VIRTUE

When I was growing up, my parents aimed to keep my brother, sister, and me in church regularly. I enjoyed the services at our church, but my favorites were the women's group that my mother led. She called it "Women of Virtue," based on the Proverbs 31 woman. As a result, I heard this passage on a regular basis. We even had jackets, shirts, bookmarks, notebooks, and other accessories designed with the virtuous woman theme. Now that I am an adult, I can admit that for the longest time I despised the Proverbs 31 woman. Each time I read about her, I inwardly rolled my eyes because she seemed like an unattainable dream that was used to make me feel bad about my shortcomings and failures.

Once, as a teenager, I was at the mall with a group of friends. One of my girlfriends was wearing a blue jean jacket that said Proverbs 31 on the back. One of the young men asked her to quote Proverbs 31. Naturally, she couldn't. The young man obnoxiously responded, "You're not a virtuous woman if you cannot quote it! You need to take that jacket off!" It was embarrassing, and I felt for my friend, but I couldn't help but think, *Ugh—as if it isn't hard enough trying to be like this woman, now we must be able to quote her chapter too?* This incident only served to strengthen my disdain for the Proverbs 31 woman.

Not until I was in my twenties did the Lord deepen my revelation about the Proverbs 31 woman. I realized she wasn't an unattainable goal but a description of what God built into women. Early one Saturday morning, I was preparing to minister at our campus ministry at Michigan State University in Lansing, Michigan. As I was in prayer, the Lord gave me a women's message called "The Glass Rose." It was a very powerful message about the value of women, and I was honored that He entrusted it to me. He began to show me that every woman is created with the same grace and anointing revealed in Proverbs 31. It is a part of our makeup as helpers. I began to burst with excitement as I realized that this virtuous woman is a blueprint of the beauty of a woman who chooses to walk with God.

This revelation changed my life, and if you grasp it, I believe it will change yours as well. Every grace this woman possessed is attainable and available to you through Jesus Christ. He died to restore us back to how God intended us to be—women functioning with multiples gifts and anointings from Him. Let's walk through this passage to see just what we are working with.

Proverbs 31

"Who can find a virtuous woman? For her price is far above rubies" (Prov. 31:10). This woman is a multi-anointed woman. The word *virtue* here means "manifestation of God's power." She is walking in the manifestation of God's anointing. She is precious and valuable. I love how the Amplified version also uses the words *capable* and *intelligent* to describe her. So many women spend their days with feelings of inadequacy when the truth is that they are worth more than precious stones.

"The heart of her husband trusts in her [with secure confidence], and he will have no lack of gain" (Prov. 3:11 AMP). This woman is graced to be trustworthy. She can listen and hear her husband while vaulting his inner most thoughts and feelings safely in her heart. That's a big deal, and I encourage you to embrace that! I don't know about you, but I like to talk. After all, I talk for a living. If I am honest, it's easy for me to get caught up in saying and sharing too much, and I dealt with quite a bit of shame as a result. My mother is naturally a quiet person, unlike me, so most of the time, I didn't even try to walk in this grace because I didn't believe I had it. However, this anointing is available to all women. Through the power of God, we can rise above our limitations and allow God to grow the character and fruits He has placed in each one of us. Regardless of your personality type, this wonderful trait is part of your package!

"She comforts, encourages, and does him only good and not evil all the days of her life" (Prov. 31:12 AMP). She is graced to be merciful. It's easy to do good when people are being good to us, but let's be real, no matter how wonderful her husband was, I am sure he had some bad days. However, we have within us the ability to do good even when the other person doesn't deserve it. That's a powerful skill because we will always have a reason to be vindictive or angry about something. People are people, and we live in a fallen world. Those temptations to hold grudges and seek vengeance will arise, but true freedom is not found in getting back at people. That is the definition of *bondage.* When we allow the actions of others to cause us to alter our standards, we are giving them keys to control our lives. No, like the virtuous woman, you are fashioned to walk in the love of God in every situation, no matter the idiosyncrasies of others.

"She looks for wool and flax and works with willing hands in delight" (Prov. 31:13 AMP). This woman is a worker. She tapped into an anointing to work. Each of us has gifts and abilities that God will use and multiply. Whether you are working in the home or on the job, you are graced with power from on high to succeed. Sometimes we find ourselves in seasons when we are tasked with less desirable jobs, but let me encourage you by reminding you that you are anointed to prosper. That grace on your life can take that not good situation and turn it into very good. This too is a part of your makeup.

"She is like the merchant ships [abounding with treasure]; she brings her [household's] food from far away" (Prov. 31:14 AMP). I love this. This woman is graced to be an ingenious shopper. She knows where to find the deals even if she must venture out to get it. She doesn't just buy anything but wisely knows how to get the best bang for her buck. *Go, girl!* Even God appreciates a woman who can shop!

"She rises also while it is still night and gives food to her household and assigns tasks to her maids" (Prov. 31:15 AMP). She is graced with the ability to manage her time wisely. Many women carry multiple tasks and responsibilities to the point that it can be overwhelming, yet God has equipped us to be efficient with our time and the delegation of tasks so that we can gracefully handle the responsibilities that come our way.

"She considers a field before she buys or accepts it [expanding her business prudently]; with her profits she plants fruitful vines in her vineyard" (Prov. 31:16 AMP). The virtuous woman is graced to be a good businesswoman. She is a producer. Whether you are starting your own business, working for someone else, volunteering your time, or managing your household, this is also a part of your package.

"She equips herself with strength [spiritual, mental, and physical fitness for her God-given task] and makes her arms strong" (Prov. 31:17 AMP). This woman is a woman of strength. One of the things that sticks out to me the most about this scripture is that this strength is intentional. She makes it her business to do what's necessary to keep herself strong spiritually, physically, and mentally. Sometimes it is easier to accept weakness when we see no reason to press toward strength. However, the virtuous woman acknowledges that God has given her a purpose and task to fulfill, and she keeps herself strong in order to fulfill it. Likewise, you are here for a reason! God has carved a path that only you can walk. Take care of yourself, build your prayer life, immerse yourself in the Word of God, cast your cares on the Lord, and honor Him in your body so that you can fulfill your great calling.

"She sees that her gain is good; her lamp does not go out, but it burns continually through the night [she is prepared for whatever lies ahead]" (Prov. 31:18 AMP). Here we see she has the grace to prepare. When we accept Jesus into our lives, He comes to live in us. He is the Good Shepherd, and the Holy Spirit leads and guides us. This woman walks in relationship with God and listens to His wisdom, which allows her to be prepared both for what she sees coming and what she doesn't. You don't have to live a life of worry and fear. Like this virtuous woman, as you seek God faithfully today, your tomorrows will be taken care of (see Matt. 3:33–34).

"She stretches out her hands to the distaff, and her hands hold the spindle [as she spins wool into thread for clothing]" (Prov. 31:18 AMP). She is a capable woman. We saw earlier that she is a gifted shopper, but I love that she is also able to take what she has and make it into something of value. She is creative, and she is skilled. Maybe you don't have everything you desire, but you too are a capable woman. Perhaps, if you put your hand to what you have, you will see that you actually have much more than you realized, and you will make something of it.

"She opens and extends her hand to the poor, and she reaches out her filled hands to the needy" (Prov. 31:20 AMP). This woman is a giver, and she is prosperous. She has the heart of God, and as a result, He can not only get blessings *to* her, but He can also get them *through* her. As Jesus tells us in the New Testament, "It is more blessed to give than to receive" (Acts 20:35).

"She does not fear the snow for her household, for all in her household are clothed in [expensive] scarlet [wool]" (Prov. 31:21 AMP). She is fearless and graced with wisdom and initiative. She is anointed for the times in which she lives, just as you are. She knows the seasons will change, so she wisely prepares her household for the future. God has given His Holy Spirit to help us see what's on the horizon and to prepare for those changes throughout the seasons of our lives.

"She makes for herself coverlets, cushions, and rugs of tapestry. Her clothing is linen, pure and fine, and purple [wool]" (Prov. 31:21 AMP). I love how this verse highlights that God celebrates and values her style. She has fashion sense and presents herself with quality, purity, and design. We all have differing ideas and preferences, but God is a creative being. He is vibrant and diverse, so celebrate who He has created you to be, and have fun being a woman. He has graced you with a style all your own.

"Her husband is known in the [city's] gates, when he sits among the elders of the land" (Prov. 31:23 AMP). When I read this verse, I think of my mother. She is the epitome of the virtuous woman. I watched as she demonstrated the strength required to be the wife of my father, a known man. He has pastored many churches nationally and presided over even more internationally. I watched as my mother was often pushed aside and overlooked. While some honored her as the first lady of our ministry, many judged her, competed with her, and disrespected her all while smiling in my father's face. However, she, like the virtuous woman, did not jump into the mud with those ignorant people but tapped into that anointing to be loving, gracious, and confident even in the face of their attacks. Not only did she handle this well, but she is also not bitter or damaged. She is as much a virtuous woman now as she was before the attacks. That grace is afforded to each one of us. Praise God.

"She makes [fine] linen garments and sells them; and supplies sashes to the merchants" (Prov. 31:24 AMP). Again we see her business skills highlighted. She turned the work of her hands into a business. Don't minimize your skills or what you have to offer. Maybe you didn't go to college, or maybe you don't run a Fortune 500 company, but God can bless you with what you have been given. Many stories exist of women who turned their so-called trivial abilities into million-dollar businesses. Maybe you could be next.

"Strength and dignity are her clothing, and her position is strong and secure; and she smiles at the future [knowing that she and her family are prepared]" (Prov. 31:25 AMP). This is a secure and confident woman. She understands where to place her value. She isn't clothed or secured by the opinions of others but by the strength and dignity that only come from a life lived in the knowledge of God. Her insecurities and fears are dimmed because she has walked in the grace and power of God in her day-to-day life. She knows who she is in Him. This too can be your testimony as you daily continue to walk with God.

"She opens her mouth in [skillful and godly] wisdom, and the teaching of kindness is on her tongue [giving counsel and instruction]" (Prov. 31:26 AMP). The virtuous woman can control her mouth! God has given us the ability to walk in self-control even in undesirable situations. Notice that she is not only wise about what comes out of her mouth but also wise about when to speak. The words we speak are powerful and have great impact, whether positive or negative. The Bible says, "Even so the tongue is a little member, and boasteth great things. Behold, how great a matter a little fire kindleth" (James 3:5).

"She looks well to how things go in her household, and does not eat the bread of idleness" (Prov. 31:27 AMP). She has a grace to keep house, and she is not lazy. Her home is clean and in order. Maybe by nature you wouldn't consider yourself to be a clean or organized person, but God has graced you with the ability to manage your home well. If you don't believe you can do it, you never will. Like this virtuous woman, you have within you what you need to do anything you set your mind and heart to. This is one of the beauties of being a woman.

"Her children rise up and call her blessed (happy, prosperous, to be admired); her husband also, and he praises her, saying, 'Many daughters have done nobly, and well [with the strength of character that is steadfast in goodness], but you excel them all'" (Prov. 31:28–29 AMP). You may be thinking, *No way has God placed all of this in me!* I know that feeling all too well, but let me triumphantly and emphatically say, *YES, HE DID!* Have you ever purchased furniture that needed to be put together? It comes with all the pieces in the box and an instruction manual showing you how they all fit together. Many times I have chosen to bypass the instruction manual and tried to figure it out on my own. In those instances, I often ended up with unused pieces and a subpar assembly. Not until sometime later, as the furniture began to fail, did I understand the importance of those instructions and the pieces I had bypassed in my haste. Likewise, you may not be operating in all the graces as the Proverbs 31 woman yet, but it's not because you don't have what it takes. Perhaps you just need to read the instruction manual, the Word of God, a little more carefully to put all the pieces into action in your life.

"Charm and grace are deceptive, and [superficial] beauty is vain, but a woman who fears the Lord [reverently worshiping, obeying, serving, and trusting Him with awe-filled respect], she shall be praised. Give her of the product of her hands, And let her own works praise her in the gates [of the city]" (Prov. 31:30–31 AMP). Beautiful woman of God, regardless of what is going on in your life or how many failures you have experienced, God has not changed His mind about you. He has not given up on His masterpiece, so don't give up on yourself. You have, right now, built into you everything you need to shine as the glorious woman He so skillfully created you to be.

Lesson Three

Protect What You Have

And when the woman saw that the tree was good for food, and that it was pleasant to the eyes, and a tree to be desired to make one wise, she took of the fruit thereof, and did eat, and gave also unto her husband with her; and he did eat (Genesis 3:6).

Hopefully in these first two lessons from Eve you have figured out that *you have it going on!* What a beautiful revelation we have discovered concerning the splendor God created in you. That's quite a crown He has put on your head. When God has created you to be this *good,* it doesn't stop there. Just ask Eve. Now that we have a better understanding of what God has granted and gifted to you, let's take some time and learn how to protect it!

You Won't Protect
What You Don't Value

Protection starts with identifying something worthy of protecting. I am convinced Eve would have been more careful about her environment if she had had a better understanding of its value. This is a principle we use in our everyday lives. If we have a nice home, we outfit it with a home security system. We put alarms on our cars, locks on our luggage, passwords on our computers, and the more technologically savvy of us may even AirTag important items. We do this because we want to protect assets that are valuable to us. Our worlds would drastically improve if we learned to value and thus protect our hearts with this same diligence, effort, and fervor. That's why it is so important to understand your value in Christ. Often, that is the determining factor in how well you guard your crown. The boundaries you set around your life can and will affect every aspect of your being. What you allow in matters. Where you go matters. What you listen to matters. Who you hang around matters.

I will never forget the day the Lord illuminated this principle to me. I was at the mall, feeling so frustrated and annoyed while trying to find a good parking space. I had been at it for over 15 minutes, looking for that perfect spot close to the door, hawking shoppers as they walked to their cars in hopes of getting their spot while side-eyeing other drivers poking around and competing to steal that spot from me. Sure, the back of the parking lot had plenty of spots available, but I wasn't interested in that walk. Around and around I went, and the more I went, the more frazzled

I became. Eventually, I ended up just where I didn't want to be: parked in the *back of the parking lot.*

As I reluctantly got out of my car and looked around, I was surprised to see that most of the cars back there were super nice. Some of them were even parked slanted across two parking spaces like they literally came to the back to park on purpose! *Who does that!?!* I wondered. *Who would park all the way back here unless they absolutely had to?* As I thought about it on my long walk to the door, I began to realize that those people parked so far away because they valued their cars. They were willing to walk a little bit farther or wait a little bit longer to keep their cars safe. The more cars in the parking lot, the greater the chance that someone dings or scratches your car. Rather than take that chance, these drivers were willing to trade the quick and convenient close-up spots for the long haul if it meant protecting their precious and expensive vehicles. There's wisdom in that. Wouldn't we all be better off if we took this approach in our lives? There's more to life than comfort and convenience.

GUARD YOUR HEART

The most important and valuable part of us needs protecting. As Proverbs tells us, "Keep and guard your heart with all vigilance and above all that you guard, for out of it flows the springs of life" (Prov. 4:23 AMPC). Guarding your heart means deciding to protect what is most important—your heart. We are not just to protect it but to protect it with all diligence, above all else that we guard. In other words, this ought to be the priority. The Bible uses the word *heart* over eight hundred times, but here the Hebrew word used for heart, *leb*, refers to the core or center of who you are, your mind, feelings, and intellect.

Perhaps Eve's first mistake was entertaining the conversation of the serpent. Never underestimate the power of suggestion. It is one of Satan's most effective tools in stealing from our lives. Eve knew what the Lord had said about that forbidden fruit. How different her life would have been if she had decided to cut the serpent off the moment his conversation contradicted what God had already said.

My favorite type of movie is the kind with a damsel in distress and a hero that swoops in and saves the day. We all love the great rescue stories, but when it comes to protecting the core of who you are, you must be your own heroine. Guarding your heart isn't something that can be peddled off to someone else; only you can play that role in your life. You must be your heart's bodyguard! Guarding your heart is the most important job you have, because "everything you do flows from it" (Prov. 4:23 NIV).

Your actions, decisions, and character are greatly affected by the condition of your heart. Satan understood that. He saw all that Eve was created to be. In fact, I am convinced he understood Eve's greatness more than she did. The serpent's role was to introduce the suggestion that God was lying to her. He argued that instead of God loving her, He was trying to hold her back and keep her from a better life. Nothing could have been further from the truth. Although Eve was magnificently created and gifted by God, she was fooled simply because the wrong person had her ear. How many times have we found ourselves in trouble as a result of listening to the wrong people?

Here is a powerful truth that, if embraced, will greatly impact you: Whoever has your ear has your life! Eve gave the serpent her ear, and in turn, he was able to steal the *zoe* life God had created for her. We see this principle also in Romans 10:9, which says that faith comes by hearing and hearing by the Word of God. What you believe in the core of who you are is based on what you have allowed yourself to continue to hear. This is such an important revelation. It gives new light and emphasis to the wisdom Solomon shared:

> *Put away from you false and dishonest speech, and willful and contrary talk put far from you. Let your eyes look right on [with fixed purpose], and let your gaze be straight before you. Consider well the path of your feet, and let all your ways be established and ordered aright. Turn not aside to the right hand or to the left; remove your foot from evil* (Proverbs 4:24–27 AMPC).

Don't Entertain the Lie

Wisdom dictates being more protective about who and what we allow to influence our lives. Eve's life is a cautionary tale of what happens when you let your guard down. The moment the serpent's communications began to contradict the truth of God's word, Eve should have put it far from her. We, like Eve, are sponges. Whatever we soak up is what will come out when the pressures of life come to squeeze us. We live in a world that continually makes suggestions to our minds. We are bombarded nonstop with negative and ungodly messages; the advancements of technology have only intensified this. So, in order to withstand the onslaught of the enemy, we must get aggressive about feeding our hearts, minds, and spirits with the truth of God's Word!

How dangerous it is to allow the opinions and philosophies of this world to be the deciding factor in all we say and do. The Bible says, "As long as the earth endures, seedtime and harvest, cold and heat, summer and winter, day and night will never cease" (Gen. 8:22 NIV). This means that the harvest you receive in your life is based on the seeds that you sow or allow to be sown into your heart. Let's not repeat Eve's mistake but learn from it. Protect your *sower!* You don't have to be bound to the lies of the enemy, regardless of who or what his lies come through. It is in your personal best interest to daily take the time to hear what God says about your life, potential, and situation.

SELF-SABOTAGE

When we listen to the lies of the enemy, we open ourselves to sabotaging our own destiny. This is what happened with Eve.

> *And when the woman saw that the tree was good for food, and that it was pleasant to the eyes, and a tree to be desired to make one wise, she took of the fruit thereof, and did eat, and gave also unto her husband with her; and he did eat* (Genesis 3:6).

Eve willingly ate to her own demise. The serpent didn't tie her up and force it down her throat. No, her self-sabotage began when instead of accepting the truth of the beauty God had created her with, she bought the lie of the enemy that she was missing something and needed to go outside of God's boundaries to get it. Perhaps the most jarring consequence of this mishap was that it didn't just affect her, but it also negatively impacted her relationship with her significant other. Eve went from honeymooning in paradise with Adam to being thrown under the bus by him as soon as God questioned him: "It was that woman you gave me..." (Gen. 3:12). To put it in modern terms, I'm guessing Adam slept on the couch that night.

Unfortunately, many women find themselves in similar situations—caught up in sin, bad relationships, depression, and torment because they are trying to attain love, peace, and acceptance outside of the will of God. Those things can only be found in Him. What Eve was looking for could never be found in the fruit from the tree of the knowledge of good and evil. Her success, peace, and joy were in the hands and within the boundaries of God. If only she had understood that, I am convinced she would have made a better choice.

Here is a powerful truth about your life: Everything you believe about yourself is stored in your heart. You are constantly creating a world around you that reflects what you believe about yourself. I've been blessed to minister to many women over the years. And no matter how much I see it, I'm still surprised when I see beautiful and amazing women who are more comfortable in dysfunction than wholeness simply because of how they view themselves.

True healing starts in the heart, and true freedom grows from protecting it.

You may have been told all your life that you are nothing or treated as if you are nothing more than body parts. You may not have been able to control the circumstances in which you were brought up as a child. But, my dear sister, regardless of what you have been through and what may have been previously sown into your heart, you don't have to stay in that position and allow that filth to negatively affect your life and decisions. Your life up to this point may have been on a path going nowhere fast, but Jesus loves you, and He died for you to remind you of who you are in Him! The noise and drama of the world can seem overwhelming, but it is not stronger than the truth of God's Word. Put God's Word first!

A RENEWED APPROACH

The Bible talks about renewing your mind, which in turn affects your heart: "And be not conformed to this world: but be ye transformed by the renewing of your mind, that ye may prove what is that good, and acceptable, and perfect, will of God" (Rom. 12:2). This takes time and effort, but it is so worth it to allow the Word of God to wash out all the damage of your past. Sometimes it's easier to stay stuck than to fight your way out, but don't allow comfort and convenience to keep you trapped without your crown. Greater things are on your horizon. Don't be like I was in that parking lot, unwilling to go that extra mile to protect my asset. Fight for your life by investing quality time in the love of God, knowing that each positive step you take is a move toward the wonderful life and influence that God has designed specifically for you.

You may say, "Well, I constantly make horrible decisions, so I deserve where I am at." Let me challenge that thought: perhaps you continue to make poor decisions because what you are choosing is in lockstep with what you believe about yourself. Change happens when you trade that darkness for the light of God's opinion concerning you. You may have had thousands of people say horrible things about you, but that's just noise. Go ahead and *turn that down!* If they didn't die for you on the cross, then they don't deserve to have the pen that writes upon your heart.

One word from God can change your entire existence—if you let it. If you choose to prioritize what He says over what they say or what you feel, then great things lie ahead in your future. Healing and restoration belong to you not because you deserve it but because Jesus died to give them to you. He made you worthy. He chose you when He had other options. So get up off that bed of self-sabotage and accept the crown God created and fashioned specifically for you. Today is a new day and a new season for you. Walk in that light and leave the darkness behind. As the apostle Peter wrote:

> *But ye are a chosen generation, a royal priest-*
> *hood, an holy nation, a peculiar people; that ye*
> *should shew forth the praises of him who hath*
> *called you out of darkness into his marvelous light*
> (1 Pet. 2:9).

Don't Leave Home Without It

Finally, my brethren, be strong in the Lord, and in the power of his might. Put on the whole armour of God, that ye may be able to stand against the wiles of the devil. For we wrestle not against flesh and blood, but against principalities, against powers, against the rulers of the darkness of this world, against spiritual wickedness in high places (Ephesians 6:10–12).

If you live on this earth, you will experience trials and tribulations, but the Word of God encourages us to be strong in Him. That's good news because He's not asking you to stand in your own power but in His. You are not in this battle alone. His might is made available to enable you to withstand every attack the enemy levels against you. God has given you His armor so that when you stand complete in it, you are sure to win.

I have a beautiful niece named Alyssa. She is the most fashionable toddler I have ever seen. I am always eager, with great anticipation, to see how my sister will dress her each time I see her. She is sure to be coordinated from head to toe. Her hair pieces, jewelry, tights, and shoes always complement each other, and occasionally she will top off her look with a bit of lip gloss and nail polish. My sister, Kristina, always decks her daughter out from head to toe every time she leaves the house. Likewise, the Word tells us to get decked out in the armor of God. You are precious cargo and worth protecting, so don't leave any piece of that armor behind.

> *Stand therefore, having your loins girt about with truth, and having on the breastplate of righteousness; and your feet shod with the preparation of the gospel of peace; above all, taking the shield of faith, wherewith ye shall be able to quench all the fiery darts of the wicked. And take the helmet of salvation, and the sword of the Spirit, which is the word of God: praying always with all prayer and supplication in the Spirit, and watching thereunto with all perseverance and supplication for all saints* (Ephesians 6:14–18).

The first piece of the armor of God mentioned here is the belt of truth. A soldier's belt would hold the entire armor in place, not allowing any part to slip or be lost. As a belt wraps around the core of the soldier, so should we be encompassed with God's truth. Trials and tribulations have a way of talking to us. Our feelings get involved, and before you know it, we find ourselves stuck in discouragement. That's why the Bible tells us to make sure we keep truth around us every day. That way, when life brings the pressure, it won't be able to penetrate our hearts and minds.

Next comes the breastplate of righteousness. Because of the blood of Jesus, we are made righteous in Him. Agreeing with that righteousness is crucial. So many women live in turmoil because they believe that's all they deserve. Many never strive for more because they feel unworthy of greater. But God's gift doesn't come to us because we have it altogether but because of His love. His sacrifice paid the price for our sins. Through repentance and forgiveness, we can boldly receive the grace we need to overcome any challenge. Because of Jesus, you were made worthy, and He wants you to wear that righteousness front and center like He does. "For He [the Lord] put on righteousness like a coat of armor..." (Isa. 59:17a AMP).

Don't forget your armored shoes shod with the gospel of peace. There's nothing like a great pair of shoes to accentuate an outfit. But more importantly, shoes protect the feet and enable them to travel long distances and through rough terrain. When you walk in the full armor of God, not even the most egregious situations can steal your peace. You don't have to be stressed out or overwhelmed by the attacks of the enemy, because the gospel provides peace even in the storm. That peace is not just for us. We are to carry that good news of Jesus all over the world. You don't have to be a preacher to spread the gospel of Jesus. His light is in you. Let it shine! Power resides in your story and hope in your testimony.

The helmet of salvation represents protection for our minds. This is crucial because the mind is the true battlefield. Many a battle has been lost between the ears, which is why the Bible encourages us to renew our minds with the Word of God (see Rom. 12:1). When it seems like fires are raging all around you, peace and comfort are available as you wash your fears away with the stability of His Word. The salvation Jesus offers is a whole-life salvation. You don't have to go crazy and lose your mind during challenging times. His love is abundant, ready, and ever-present in any situation you face.

Time to break out the bling with the sword of the spirit!

For the word of God is living and active and full of power [making it operative, energizing, and effective]. It is sharper than any two-edged sword, penetrating as far as the division of the soul and spirit [the completeness of a person], and of both joints and marrow [the deepest parts of our nature], exposing and judging the very thoughts and intentions of the heart (Hebrews 4:12 AMP).

The Word of God is strong enough to defeat anything, so always keep it with you.

Finally, we find power in prayer. Paul encourages us to pray not only for ourselves but also for others.

Therefore let us [with privilege] approach the throne of grace [that is, the throne of God's gracious favor] with confidence and without fear, so that we may receive mercy [for our failures] and find [His amazing] grace to help in time of need [an appropriate blessing, coming just at the right moment] (Hebrews 4:16 AMP).

What an honor it is to go before the King of kings and the Lord of lords confidently. We find safety and comfort in knowing that He hears us and answers us.

Beware of Peer Pressure

Now the serpent was more subtil than any beast of the field which the Lord God had made. And he said unto the woman, Yea, hath God said, Ye shall not eat of every tree in the garden? (Genesis 3:1).

I grew up in a Christian home. My parents graduated from Rhema Bible Training Center in 1978 and shortly after started Word of Faith Christian Center in Detroit, Michigan. Life as a pastor's kid had its ups and its downs. Thankfully, the good outweighed the bad. But one thing I was always aware of was that my actions could have greater impact than those of the average parishioner. I didn't like that people put pressure on my siblings and me, especially in our teenage years, as if they expected us to be adults while still in our youth. Nevertheless, my parents were very clear in their guidelines for how we were to govern ourselves. We were to honor God in our hearts and actions and we were to live as responsible contributors to our community. For the most part, I strived to live up to those standards. I found it easier to do in my younger years. By the time I got to high school, it was more challenging.

My parents enrolled me in a Christian high school where I made friends quickly. I've always been a social person, so settling into a new environment was fairly easy for me. Each year, at the top of the fall school term, our school required us to sign a pledge to ourselves and to God that we would honor God in our bodies by not engaging in immoral practices. One of those highlighted practices was underage drinking. The penalty for violating this pledge was expulsion from school, so it was a big deal. I watched some kids struggle within themselves to make such a pledge, but for me it was easy. I never had the desire to drink alcohol because I understood the dangers of it. In addition, no one around me or in my household drank alcohol, so it was not a temptation for me. Therefore, I made that commitment each year not only to the school but also to my parents. I had every intention of keeping my commitment, but sadly, at the age of 16, I found myself breaking my pledge while hanging out in the basement of a friend's home.

As I look back, I still struggle to believe that I gave in to that. *What was my problem?* I clearly remember the conversation I had with my parents when I returned home smelling of alcohol and feeling incredibly guilty. This wasn't like me at all. I found myself in my fair share of trouble, but not with alcohol, and certainly not after I had made a commitment to abstain from it. But there I was, giving in to peer pressure, as so many of us do. My friends and I had found some open liquor in my friend's home, and someone suggested that we should drink it for fun. I immediately refused, but as I watched my friends, one by one, partaking in this silly practice, my resolve began to weaken. I grabbed the bottle and chugged it as my friends chanted my last name, "Butler, Butler, Butler, Butler!" As a preacher's kid, I was thought of as the goody-two-shoes of the bunch, and it brought great delight to my companions to see me step outside of those standards.

You may be thinking, *This is no big deal. This is just what teenagers do.* Sure, this story is a snapshot of seemingly normal behavior from a kid wanting to please her friends. But peer pressure doesn't end with the teenage years. Many men and women still govern their lives not by their own personal standards but by the pressures and expectations of others. We even see this in the life of Eve. She knew what was right; we know that because she voiced it to the serpent. Yet she allowed prolonged conversation, consideration, and pressure to weaken her resolve. Before she and Adam sinned, the serpent was not like a snake today. He did not crawl on his belly before he was cursed (see Gen. 3:14). We can safely assume that the serpent was more attractive during the time when he had this conversation with Eve.

Whether we want to admit it or not, it can be difficult to avoid the negative effects of other people's opinions. Our world is lacking a great many things, but it is not lacking opinions. You can hardly go one step without being bombarded by someone else's thoughts and ideas, whether through newspapers, magazines, television shows, movies, social media, family, friends, colleagues or classmates. Alarmingly, in today's culture, if your opinions don't line up with the majority opinion of the day, you can find yourself subject to censorship and cancellation. In order to withstand the pressures of other people's opinions, you must be intentional and wise in your dealings with them.

BEAUTIFUL PEOPLE

And God said, Let us make man in our image, after our likeness: and let them have dominion over the fish of the sea, and over the fowl of the air, and over the cattle, and over all the earth, and over every creeping thing that creepeth upon the earth. So God created man in his own image, in the image of God created he him; male and female created he them. And God blessed them, and God said unto them, Be fruitful, and multiply and replenish the earth, and subdue it: and have dominion over the fish of the sea, and over the fowl of the air, and over every living thing that moveth upon the earth (Genesis 1:26–28).

God loves people, and He is big on relationship. After all, He created Eve so that Adam would not be alone. We see God's heart for fellowship here at the beginning of humankind when He told them to be fruitful and multiply. In essence, He was saying, "Make more people." Often, I have asked myself, *Why does God continue to engage with humankind? Why didn't He turn us into robots that have no choice but to follow Him? After the betrayals of humankind, what is God getting out of all of this?* When I was in college, many of the dissenting views about God seemed to be centered around this idea. Why would He even allow us to be here with a choice? The answer is quite simple. He values fellowship. It is very difficult to have a meaningful conversation with a baby. Many stay-at-home moms can attest to the fact that, while they love their babies, they look forward to engaging in adult conversation. Conversing with someone who is on your level is fulfilling. God created us in His image and in His likeness to be able to have meaningful fellowship.

The psalmist wrote,

> *What is man that You are mindful of him, And the son of [earthborn] man that You care for him? Yet You have made him a little lower than God, and You have crowned him with glory and honor* (Psalm 8:4–5 AMP).

God could have pushed humankind to the side and started over with a new species, yet He didn't. He still sees beautiful people. He has crowned us and welcomed us into His throne room to worship and converse with Him. He has given us the gift of choice because He made us in His class, and kings don't force other kings to do anything. The ability to choose to love God is an honor, not a curse. He openly communes with us and grants us access to the work of His hand and the majesty of His creation because He believes in us. God created the world with a vision and His word, and when He turned over the world to Adam and Eve, He did so in anticipation of seeing what they would cultivate and create. Humankind has come a long way from God's original intent, but God's heart for more people has not changed.

Jesus commissioned His disciples:

> *Go ye therefore, and teach all nations, baptizing them in the name of the Father, and of the Son, and of the Holy Ghost: Teaching them to observe all things whatsoever I have commanded you: and, lo, I am with you always, even unto the end of the world. Amen* (Matthew 28:19–20).

Even in what is often referred to as the Great Commission, we see God empowering us to go out and bring in *more people*. Likewise, in the Gospel of John, we again see God's desire to have as many people as possible with Him when He says, "Whosoever believes in him should not perish, but have everlasting life" (John 3:16). He made it so easy, enabling even the simplest among us to be able to commune with Him eternally.

Jesus longs for *more people*. In Matthew 18, He highlighted one of the benefits of *more people*:

> *Again I say unto you, That if two of you shall agree on earth as touching any thing that they shall ask, it shall be done for them of my Father which is in heaven. For where two or three are gathered together in my name, there am I in the midst of them* (Matthew 18:19–20).

Great power is made available when God's people come together in unity. The author of Hebrews put it this way:

Let us hold fast the profession of our faith without wavering; (for he is faithful that promised;) and let us consider one another to prove unto love and to good works: not forsaking the assembling of ourselves together, as the manner of some is; but exhorting one another: and so much the more, as ye see the day approaching (Hebrews 10:23–25).

God wants us to spend time with people, so much so that He commands us to gather more (and not less) the closer we get to the return of Christ. We were not created to be isolated on an island. Just as God desires fellowship, we also need other people in our lives. But with *more people* come *more opinions.* If God intends our lives to include other people, then learning how to love people while being *free* from people is paramount to obtaining a successful life.

LOVE THYSELF

Master, which is the great commandment in the law? Jesus said unto him, Thou shalt love the Lord thy God with all thy heart, and with all thy soul, and with all thy mind. This is the first and great commandment. And the second is like unto it, Thou shalt love thy neighbor as thyself. On these two commandments hang all the law and the prophets (Matthew 22:36–40).

Here in Matthew, Jesus points out the two commandments we are to live by: (1) Love God, and (2) Love people. Loving God means opening your heart and mind to Him and allowing His truth to become your truth. However, I want to focus on the second commandment. Not only does it say to love your neighbor, but it says to love your neighbor *as yourself*. In order to love people, you must first love yourself. A direct connection exists between how you love yourself and how you treat other people. Many people struggle in loving other people because they don't love themselves. As a result, their relationship choices and boundaries reflect that imbalance and brokenness.

When I finally understood that the plan of God for my life included full-time ministry, even though I desired God's best, I almost walked away from His plan because I didn't like people. Growing up as a preacher's kid, I had many negative experiences with some parishioners that I attributed to all of them. *Why would I want to sacrifice my life to help people I don't like?* But the real question was, Why was I so opposed to "church people"?

Many wonderful people had loved me, prayed for me, and intended the best for me, and they did outweigh the negative folks. So many times, faithful members of our church family spoke love and hope over me. However, as I have previously mentioned, for many reasons I did not like myself. As a result, I took no account of the many blessings I experienced because I did not believe the compliments I received. It was so much easier for me to hold on to and focus on the grumblings of a critical few because their words were more familiar to the narrative in my head. That negativity received all my time and effort because it reminded me of the dark reality of what I thought of myself. Thus, the disdain and bitterness I had for myself were the emotions I attached to all "church people." Even worse, I gave extra weight to the opinions of those negative people by becoming tangled up in seeking their approval or distracted by trying to prove them wrong.

Thankfully, I can say now that I have learned to love and appreciate all of God's people, but that did not happen by accident. I had to make an intentional effort to learn to first love myself. Perhaps my greatest fear was that my haters were right and that I was unlovable. The apostle John wrote, "There is no fear in love; but perfect love casteth out fear: because fear hath torment. He that fears is not made perfect in love. We love him, because he first loved us" (1 John 4:18–19). My problem was that I was trying to find something good in me to love. True freedom began to permeate by heart when I accepted the truth that God loved me as I was, just as He also loves you. Before I even knew Him or could improve any of my flaws, He valued and chose me. What a liberating truth.

You don't have to become what the world deems as lovable for God to love you; He already does. He loves you too much to leave you unchanged. The Bible tells us to renew our minds to the Word of God, which means we should adopt His views about us, not the views dictated by our past or present (see Rom. 12:2). You can love yourself because God loves you. You can find value in yourself because God calls you valuable. You can believe in yourself because the Creator of the universe, who knows all things, believes in you.

The trouble in relationships comes when we put pressure on other people to make us feel worthy. That was never their job. You cannot expect people to fill God's place in your life. Operating like that causes us to elevate other people's thoughts and opinions to an unhealthy place in our lives. You must first settle, within yourself, your value in God and learn to love yourself. The measure of love, respect, honor, and forgiveness you afford to yourself is what you will have to give to others.

PEOPLE PLEASING

So many bad decisions are a result of trying to please other people. This has been a major issue in my life. Very early in life, I attached my value to the praises of other people. As a result, I spent much of my life without healthy boundaries. It got so bad, at one point, that if you asked me what I wanted, I could not tell you unless my answer was validated by someone else. If people were impressed by me, then I was okay, but if they were silent or lackluster in their opinion of me, I felt lost. It was as if I was living my life chained to a never-ending roller coaster—exhausted and nauseated. I gave away my power in exchange for the fleeting applause of people.

My journey toward freedom began the day the Lord showed me the root cause of my need to please. Because I believed I was unlovable, I resorted to trying to do things for people to *make* them love me. I worried that if I didn't do what others wanted, then I would be alone and unhappy. Praise God that is not the truth—not for me or for you! The Bible says, "When a man's ways please the Lord, he makes even his enemies to be at peace with him" (Prov. 16:7 NKJV). If pleasing the Lord means my enemies find peace with me, then surely everyone in between will be taken care of as well. When you decide to focus on walking with God, everything else that matters will find its way to you (see Matt. 6:33).

STOP COMPARING

Making comparison is making a judgment about what you *think* you know. When you compare yourself to other people, you do so without all the facts. The invention of social media has intensified this phenomenon in today's culture. While social media provides views into the lives of others, it does not communicate the whole story. Yet many people find themselves discontented because they compare the totality of their lives to the mere snapshots of other's lives online. Jesus died to give you access to *zoe* life. Don't waste His sacrifice by competing with others. God gives enough grace for each one of us.

About comparison, Paul wrote, "For we dare not make ourselves of the numbers or compare ourselves with some that commend themselves: but they measuring themselves by themselves, and comparing themselves among themselves, are not wise" (2 Cor. 10:12). One of the most effective ways to place a limiter on your life is to compare yourself to other people. Comparisons are crippling for many reasons. Comparison can cause one to pridefully elevate oneself.

> *Two men went up to the temple to pray, one a Pharisee and the other a tax collector. The Pharisee stood and prayed thus with himself, "God, I thank You that I am not like other men—extortioners,*

71

unjust, adulterers, or even as this tax collector. I fast twice a week; I give tithes of all that I possess." And the tax collector, standing afar off, would not so much as raise his eyes to heaven, but beat his breast, saying, "God, be merciful to me a sinner!" I tell you, this man went down to his house justified rather than the other; for everyone who exalts himself will be humbled, and he who humbles himself will be exalted (Luke 18:10–14 NKJV).

The Pharisee by profession held a nobler position in comparison with the tax collector, and as he noted, he had lived his life according to the laws of God. However, as he compared himself to the tax collector, the Bible says he prayed with *himself.* On the other hand, the tax collector found right standing with God because his eyes were on himself instead of pridefully competing with others.

Comparisons also serve as a distraction from the purpose and plan for your life. Eve fell for that when the serpent compared her to God, changing her focus. Instead, we must keep our focus on God's call for us:

But none of these things move me; nor do I count my life dear to myself, so that I may finish my race with joy, and the ministry which I received from the Lord Jesus, to testify to the gospel of the grace of God (Acts 20:24 NKJV).

God has given each of us our own purpose. Run your race and finish strong. When you are living out your calling in God, you don't have time to be concerned with what other people are or are not doing.

Comparison is also the death of contentment. It produces an ungrateful heart. The Bible says that "godliness with contentment is great gain" (1 Tim. 6:6). Wishing for other people's gifts and talents not only subtracts from your life, but it devalues the gift God has given you. Comparisons open your life up to covetousness, jealousy, and envy, and they will disqualify you from the future God has ordained for you. We see this in Genesis 4 with the story of Adam and Eve's sons Cain and Abel. Both brothers presented their offerings to the Lord, but only Abel's was accepted.

> *And the Lord said unto Cain, Why art thou wroth? and why is they countenance fallen? If thou doest well, shalt thou not be accepted? and if thou doest not well, sin lieth at the door. And unto thee shall be his desire, and thou shalt rule over him. And Cain talked with Abel his brother: and it came to pass, when they were in the field, that Cain rose up against Abel his brother, and slew him* (Genesis 4:6–8)

Cain's offering had nothing to do with Abel. He could have repented, made an adjustment, and continued in God. Yet, in his comparison, he allowed jealousy and envy to lead him to slay his brother. He took a bad situation and made it worse. The end result:

> *And now art thou cursed from the earth, which hath opened her mouth to receive thy brother's blood from thy hand; When thou tillest the ground, it shall not henceforth yield unto thee her*

strength; a fugitive and a vagabond shalt thou be in the earth (Genesis 4:11–12).

FOOLISH INTERACTIONS

One of the greatest skills you can have in these last days is knowing how to deal with foolishness. We all encounter foolishness from time to time, whether through people, situations, or our own lapses in judgment. It's fair to say that Eve was dealing with foolishness with that serpent, and because she didn't handle it well, she paid a hefty price. As Eve quickly learned, it is dangerous to entertain a fool. The Bible says, "He who walks with wise men will be wise, but the companion of fools will be destroyed" (Prov. 13:20 NKJV). Avoiding the pressures of a fool can prevent a lot of pain, sorrow, and heartache. "Go from the presence of a foolish man, when you do not perceive in him the lips of knowledge" (Prov. 14:7 NKJV).

An important key to surviving foolish interactions is the ability to recognize foolishness in operation. It's clear that Eve didn't comprehend the foolishness of the serpent, or she would have exited that situation quickly and saved her own life. Likewise, many have gotten caught up in bad situations and relationships because they didn't recognize the foolishness surrounding them. It's not always easy to identify a fool. Like the serpent, the devil uses subtle tactics to avoid detection. However, the Bible provides great wisdom for helping us to expose a fool.

Let's look at a few of the identifying characteristics of a fool as listed in the Bible. First, "The fool says in his heart,

'There is no God.' They are corrupt, and their ways are vile; there is no one who does good" (Prov. 53:1 NIV). When a person or situation fails to recognize God, that is a clear sign that you are dealing with a fool. Second, "A fool has no delight in understanding, But in expressing his own heart" (Prov. 18:2 NKJV). Everyone has their opinions based on their own personal perspectives, but when a person is not open to the truth of the Word of God, they are indeed operating in foolishness. Third, "To do evil is like sport to a fool, but a man of understanding has wisdom" (Prov. 10:23 NKJV). When people embrace evil and celebrate folly, they are acting as a fool.

Fourth, "In the mouth of the foolish is a rod of pride: but the lips of the wise shall preserve them" (Prov. 14:3). Any-time the circumstances, people, or reports elevate them-selves above God's Word on any subject, pride is in action, and it always leads to a fall. Do not elevate a fool in your life or you will limit the blessings of God in your life. Even well-meaning people and those we love can yield them-selves to foolish thinking from time to time. In order to keep that gorgeous crown on your head, learn to identify it and remove yourself from it. Others may not understand those choices, but preservation of your peace is worth more than their opinions about you.

THROW THAT TREE INTO THE SEA

Perhaps the biggest trap that can arise as a result of fool-ish interactions is the temptation to live in offense. We all have had foolish encounters that have caused harm, but forgiveness is vitally important. Forgiveness is not about whether the offending party deserves it; it is about freedom for the injured. When you hold on to past offenses, you allow that person to continue hurting you. Many people hold grudges, thinking they are hurting the offending party, but they are really hurting themselves. Unforgiveness is like drinking poison and hoping it kills the other person. Jesus said:

> *Take heed to yourselves: If thy brother trespass against thee, rebuke him; and if he repent, forgive him. And if he trespass against thee seven times in a day, and seven times in a day turn again to thee, saying, I repent; thou shalt forgive him. And the apostles said unto the Lord, Increase our faith. And the Lord said, If ye had the faith as a grain of mustard seed, ye might say unto this sycamine tree, Be thou plucked up by the root, and be thou planted in the sea; and it should obey you* (Luke 17:3–6).

I can understand why the disciples asked Jesus to increase their faith. After all, what He said is still tough to swallow today. In fact, it seems downright unfair. Without revelation into the heart of Jesus here, it can be easy to feel victimized by the idea of forgiving those that have hurt us repeatedly. However, looking more closely at verse 6, we see that Jesus said that if we have even the tiniest amount of faith, we can remove that sycamine tree out of our lives. The question is, *faith in what?* Faith in the fact that this commandment is for our own good because Jesus loves us. We see that in

Jesus' use of the sycamine tree. To grasp the full scope of this wisdom, we need to understand the significance of that species of tree.

Sycamine trees were known to have very large root structures. They were very difficult to remove because the roots went so deep. Even when they were cut at the base, they would often resurface again and again. The wood from a sycamine tree was the preferred choice for building caskets and coffins in those days because it grew quickly and in any environment, which made it easily accessible. It also grew the best in dry conditions. The fruit of a sycamine tree was so bitter that it could not be eaten whole but only nibble by nibble. Although the fruit resembled the sweet fruit of a mulberry tree, which the rich partook of, sycamine fruit was in fact so bitter that only the very poor ate it. Last, sycamine trees were pollinated by the sting of wasps. *Selah.*

This clearly shows us why Jesus was adamant about forgiveness! When you wallow in bitterness and unforgiveness, your life resembles the sycamine tree. Satan would love to deeply root all of that pain and anger into the core of who you are so that no matter how much you try to cut it, it will always grow back. He wants to build your casket with the pain of your past and bury your God-given potential in it. He wants you to be poor in spirit, just like the fruit of the sycamine tree, and he will continually send wasps to sting you to keep producing bitterness in your life. It's up to you to stop that madness.

Whatever pain you have experienced in the past, let it go. Release it in faith that God is able to make it right. Don't allow what others have done to you to pressure you into letting your life become dry as a desert. Throw that tree into the sea and unbury the potential that foolish encounters have attempted to steal from you. May this word from Isaiah be true for you:

> *Instead of your [former] shame you will have a double portion; and instead of humiliation your people will shout for joy over their portion. Therefore in their land they will possess double [what they have forfeited]; everlasting joy will be theirs* (Isaiah 61:7 AMP).

Lesson Five

Looks Can Be Deceiving

And when the woman saw that the tree was good for food, and that it was pleasant to the eyes, and a tree to be desired to make one wise, she took of the fruit thereof, and did eat, and gave also unto her husband with her; and he did eat (Genesis 3:6).

MORE THAN MEETS THE EYE

One of my fondest memories growing up was Saturday morning breakfast with my siblings. Usually, during the week, my mother was very strict about what we were allowed to eat. However, occasionally on the weekends we were allowed to have sugary cereals like Frosted Flakes or Fruit Loops. *YUM!* It was always a welcome change from the usual oatmeal or shredded wheat. One of the best things about the sugar cereal was that it usually contained some sort of cool toy in the box. My all-time favorite was the Secret Spy Decoder Lens. This toy had two parts, a special set of secret pages and a secret decoder lens. The secret decoder pages had clues on them that helped you solve a mystery. However, if you looked at the pages with your natural eye, they didn't appear to have anything of value. In fact, if you weren't careful, you could end up throwing them away because they seemed useless. Only a secret spy like me or my siblings knew there was more than meets the eye. We knew that the only way to crack the case was to look at the pages through the secret decoder lens. The natural eye just wouldn't cut it. That sounds a little like real life. Too often we are fooled by something that looks one way but then turns out to be something completely different.

Certainly that was the case on that fateful day in the garden of Eden. Here's a lesson that seems simple yet is so profound: *Not everything that looks good is good.* Looks can certainly be deceiving. It's easy to understand how Eve fell into that trap in the garden. Let's be real; it would be much easier to avoid mess-ups if the temptation looked like death in the first place. If that super-fine man had visible horns or a devil's tail, then surely one would easily avoid that dysfunctional relationship. If that bad-news friend came with a sign stamped on her forehead that said, "I will lead you into big trouble," dodging that drama would be the clear choice. However, that's not how the enemy works. Temptation rarely ever presents itself as what it really is. Otherwise, it would not be tempting.

Eve was looking at deadly fruit, but it looked good. Not only did it look good, but the Bible also says it looked desirable. It certainly seemed like the serpent had a point. How could something that looked so good turn out to be so bad? Perhaps what was really missing was the secret decoder lens.

WHO DO YOU TRUST?

I've read about trusting the Lord in Proverbs 3 at least a thousand times.

> *Trust in the Lord with all thine heart; and lean not unto thine own understanding. In all thy ways acknowledge him, and he shall direct thy paths. Be not wise in thine own eyes: fear the Lord, and depart from evil. It shall be health to thy navel, and marrow to thy bones* (Proverbs 3:5–8).

If you grew up in church or around someone who loves the Lord, you have most likely encountered this powerful passage as well. In my own life, I have found that it has not always been easy to follow this advice, not because God isn't trustworthy, but because at times I have given in to my own fears, thoughts, and feelings. The promises of God are yes and amen, but they aren't always tangible or visible when we want them to be. The Bible tells us, in Isaiah 55:8, that God's thoughts and ways are higher than ours. On the one hand, I openly celebrate that. But on the other hand, I have found that it can be challenging when what the Lord is saying doesn't look like what I want to hear or see. Have you ever been there?

Perhaps my best life example of this is my lengthy journey toward marriage. One of my greatest desires had always been to be a wife and a mother. Honestly, it wasn't something that I ever imagined would be a struggle. One of the scriptures I patterned my life after was, "Delight yourself also in the Lord, and He shall give you the desires of your heart" (Ps. 37:4 NKJV). I lived a rock-solid life for God in my 20s, traveling and preaching the gospel of Jesus Christ and helping others to discover His great love for them. But by the time I hit my mid-30s, was still single, did not see any viable options, and had experienced some painful rejections, I started to have doubts.

Coming home to an empty apartment day after day, I didn't feel like God loved me or even cared about me. I was battling through a cancer diagnosis at the time as well, which meant multiple treatments and doctors' visits that seemed to further highlight that I was alone and unwanted. It just felt so unfair. I had chosen to live a chaste life before God as a single woman, which meant abstaining from sex and other compromising situations, but it seemed to me that all the women I saw who weren't living that standard had their men and their happily-ever-afters. It felt like the joke was on me. Needless to say, that forbidden fruit started to look pretty good.

I found myself saying things like, "Maybe marriage just isn't in the cards for me." "Maybe I'm just too big and not attractive enough." "Maybe I'm just better off alone." My relationship status had become my focus, and I had allowed what I was seeing and feeling to become more real to me than what God had promised concerning my life. While that is so easy to do, especially in areas we really care about, it is also very dangerous. Satan was able to dethrone Eve because her trust was misplaced, and he will gladly do the same to us if we allow him. He will parade counterfeits and set traps that look the part but lead to destruction. Many times, I came close to settling and forfeiting my crown—until the day I truly realized how great God's love for me is and how much I can trust Him.

In Proverbs 3:5–8, it says:

> *Trust God from the bottom of your heart; don't try to figure out everything on your own. Listen for God's voice in everything you do, everywhere you go; he's the one who will keep you on track. Don't assume that you know it all. Run to God! Run from evil! Your body will glow with health, your very bones will vibrate with life* (MSG).

I remember the day I finally accepted that truth. I felt an overwhelming sense of peace. The stress of trying to figure it out myself—or the fear that something was wrong with me—dissipated in the arms of a loving God who reminded me that He had my back. It wasn't a question of whether God would take care of me but of whether I was going to trust Him. I didn't just need to trust that God would bring someone for me, but I needed to also allow Him to grow me up and prepare me for what I couldn't see at that time—my wonderful husband, Lee.

It is so easy to get caught up, like Eve, in what you see, but perhaps it's time to upgrade your lenses. If you don't trade in those natural views for a heavenly one, your life will seem depressing. Life will certainly throw situations your way that appear as if all hope is gone, but when you take another look with heavenly lenses, that hopeless situation can take on a whole different view.

THE ALTERNATE VIEW

And when the disciples saw Him walking on the sea, they were troubled, saying, "It is a ghost!" And they cried out for fear. But immediately Jesus spoke to them, saying, "Be of good cheer! It is I; do not be afraid." And Peter answered Him and said, "Lord, if it is You, command me to come to You on the water." So He said, "Come." And when Peter had come down out of the boat, he walked on the water to go to Jesus. But when he saw that the wind was boisterous, he was afraid; and beginning to sink he cried out, saying, "Lord, save me!" And immediately Jesus stretched out His hand and caught him, and said to him, "O you of little faith, why did you doubt?" And when they got into the boat, the wind ceased (Matthew 14:26–32 NKJV).

One of the most popular stories in the Bible is that of Peter walking on the water. I admire Peter's spunk; he was the only one who asked to get out of the boat. Despite his falter, what Peter accomplished was a miracle. But let's take a look at why that miracle was cut short. Many blessings are available when you get out of the boat of comfort and stretch forth to Jesus. Everything that Peter needed to defy gravity was present the moment Jesus spoke that word, *come.* The interesting thing is, we know Peter experienced power because he did walk on the water. Sometimes we think, *Lord, if I can just experience Your power, I will never doubt again.* But just as it did with Peter, doubt can creep in even after you've already been walking in your miracle. I can personally attest to that.

Several years into the ministry, I had overcome much fear and had grown mightily in the preaching grace that God had placed on my life. It was almost a miracle for me to be able to say that I had become comfortable behind the pulpit, which was something I never thought would be the case. I had several successful messages under my belt and was excited about the future. Then one day, a compliment turned into a mountain of fear in my life. I had just finished ministering a message that went over very well. It was anointed and powerful. Usually when I am done preaching, I gather my things and head straight home. But on this day, I decided to stick around and talk to the people. It was amazing to hear the impact the message had had on those I conversed with. They cried; they raved; they celebrated. I heard marvelous testimonies and received so much encouragement. Over the next few days, my email was filled with even more testimonies and praise, all as a result of that one message.

At first, I was thankful that God had allowed me to minister that word and that He had anointed it. I surely did not take that for granted. However, over the next several days, that gratitude turned to fear. You see, the more compliments I received, the more I began to worry about my next message. *How could I ever top this one?* So many people were expressing their excitement over hearing my next message that I became sure I could never deliver anything as effective as what they had experienced through my last message. I had forgotten that my ministry gift wasn't through my power but was a result of the grace of God on my life. God does not run out of power! Here I was ready to quit the ministry so that I could leave on a high note, simply because I took my eyes off Jesus and bought the lie of the enemy.

Satan presented an alternate view of my situation just like he did with Peter and with Eve in the garden. Make no mistake about it, he will always present a contradicting view of God's blessings in your life in an attempt to short-circuit them. Peter had indeed experienced the power of God in operation those first few steps, but when that wind became boisterous, he had the choice of two perspectives to adopt: the perspective of faith or that of fear. You will not always be able to control what is going on around you, but you can control the view you decide to accept about your situation. In Peter's case, the wind stopped as soon as they got back into the boat, which shows us that the wind's purpose was to stop that miracle. The next time you are tempted to put on those glasses of doubt, remember that the thief never comes for an empty house. That temptation is there because you are right where you are supposed to be. Let go of the fear and flourish in the grace of God.

THE EYE OF FAITH

In Hebrews 11:6, it says:

> *But without faith it is impossible to please him:*
> *for he that cometh to God must believe that he is,*
> *and that he is a rewarder of them that diligently*
> *seek him.*

I don't know what your world looks like today. I don't understand all of the challenges you are facing. But I do know one thing: No situation is too far gone that God cannot turn it around if you trust and believe in Him. God specializes in great comeback stories. The Bible is filled with story after story after story of lives that looked hopeless but turned into great triumphs. Consider Mary, the mother of Jesus. It looked like she had been fooling around on her fiancé, and I am sure some people probably gossiped about that. But in reality, God had chosen her to carry His Son, Jesus Christ, who would save the world (see Luke 1:28-31).

The children of Israel looked as if they were trapped at the Red Sea and would surely be killed by the Egyptians. But God did the unthinkable. He parted the sea so they could safely cross on dry land (see Exod. 14). Then there's Joseph, who seemed to be plagued with bad luck, from his brothers' attempt to murder him to his boss's wife's lies about him. But God turned it all around and made him second-in-command in all of Egypt (see Gen. 41:46). How about Job, who lost everything, to the point that his own wife told him to just curse God and die, but God gave him double for all his trouble, and he came out twice as blessed (see Job 42:10).

Let's not forget about Abraham and Sarah who were old and decrepit, but God birthed a nation through them (see Gen. 21). Daniel looked like lion food, but the Lord shut the mouths of the beasts, and he came out unharmed (see Dan. 6). Shadrach, Meshach, and Abednego looked like BBQ when faced with that fiery furnace, yet they came out unsinged and thus introduced the true and living God to an entire nation (see Dan. 3). Jonah certainly looked like fish food, but God gave him another chance, and he completed his assignment from the Lord. As a result, many repented and were saved from destruction (see Jonah 1–3). David was disgraced by the horrible choices he made with Bathsheba, and they lost a baby as a result. However, in His mercy, God blessed them with more children, including Solomon, the wisest man to walk the face of the earth (see 2 Sam. 12:24).

Noah looked like a crazy man, ridiculed and scorned, yet he survived and thrived in a worldwide flood (see Gen. 6–9). Samson seemed weak after Delilah's betrayal, yet even at his end, God restored his strength so that he defeated more enemies in his death than he had in his entire life (see Judg. 16). For the adulterous woman in John 8, her life seemed like it was over due to her mistakes. People were ready to stone her, but Jesus forgave her and gave her another chance at life. In Mark 5, Jairus's daughter looked dead, but Jesus raised her up. The woman with the issue of blood seemed hopeless, but Jesus not only healed her but also made her whole (see Mark 5:25). In John 11, it looked as if Lazarus was long gone; his body had even begun to stink. But Jesus opened the tomb and called him back to life. In Acts 28, Paul looked as if he would succumb to a poisonous snake bite, but with the power of God, he shook that viper off and felt no harm.

I could go on and on, but I would be amiss not to mention the greatest comeback story of all time—Jesus! He looked doomed on that cross. He seemed defeated in that grave, but on the third day He arose with all power and might (see Matt. 28). His is the victory of all victories.

There is no reason your story can't be the same. Do yourself a favor and trade in those dusty lenses of depression, fear, and hopelessness for that secret decoder lens called the eye of faith. God doesn't play favorites, which means there's a victory with your name on it. Don't lose sight of that; don't throw away your hope. God has given you the Word to decode the attempts of the enemy. What was meant for your harm will turn out for your good. God is not surprised by your circumstances or caught off guard by your weaknesses. But He will use those things to show Himself strong in your life.

If you really want to get to that next level, don't wait until everything looks good to celebrate. Shout now! Rejoice now! Sing now! Dance now! The God of the universe has not given up on you, so don't give up on yourself. Faith in God releases His power into your circumstances to do the impossible, the inconceivable, and the unimaginable. The bigger the battle, the greater the testimony. Beautiful woman of God, the best is certainly yet to come. As Paul the apostle wrote, "But thanks be to God, which giveth us the victory through our Lord Jesus Christ" (1 Cor. 15:57).

Lesson Six

See the Bigger Picture

And the Lord God said, Behold, the man is become as one of us, to know good and evil: and now, lest he put forth his hand, and take also of the tree of life, and eat, and live forever: Therefore the Lord God sent him forth from the garden of Eden, to till the ground from whence he was taken (Genesis 3:22–23).

One of most powerful things we possess is our ability to choose. Your choice is your superpower. It has a great effect on the quality and reality of your life. Simply put, what you are dealing with today is a result of what you sowed yesterday. Eve found herself stripped of the glory of God and escorted out of the garden of Eden because of the choice she made to disobey God. We've all been there, stuck in the results of our own bad decisions.

> *Do not be deceived and deluded and misled; God will not allow Himself to be sneered at (scorned, disdained, or locked by mere pretensions or professions, or by His precepts being set aside.) [He inevitably deludes himself who attempts to delude God.] For whatever a man sows, that and that only is what he will reap. For he who sows to his own flesh (lower nature, sensuality) will from the flesh reap decay and ruins and destruction, but he who sows to the Spirit will from the Spirit reap eternal life. And let us not lose heart and grow weary and faint in acting nobly and doing right, for in due time and at the appointed season we shall reap, if we do not loosen and relax our courage and faint* (Galatians 6:7–9 AMPC).

Clearly, Eve was intrigued by the idea of having intimate knowledge of both good and evil, so much so that she partook of the fruit and gave it to her man. I imagine, in that moment, it seemed like a reasonable decision. After all, it didn't seem like the serpent had any reason to lie, and the fruit itself looked harmless and tasty. I imagine her thinking, *Why would God put something that looks so yummy in the garden if He didn't really mean for us to eat it?* Just like Eve, we get into trouble in our lives when we narrowly judge a situation by our own limited view. In order to have God's best, we must learn to look past our flesh and see the bigger picture.

NO VISION, NO FUTURE

Vision is incredibly important. "Where there is no vision, the people perish: but he that keepeth the law, happy is he" (Prov. 29:18). If you've ever been to a job interview, you may have been asked this question, "Where do you see yourself in the next five years?" Employers ask that question because they understand vision. They recognize that if you have a vision for something, then you will begin to organize your life, behavior, thoughts, and time accordingly. Discipline follows vision. An employer knows that if an employee's vision is to rise through the ranks of the company, that likely means the employee will work hard to be productive in order to qualify for those promotions. The same applies to our everyday lives. Your vision is like a magnet; it will draw your desires to you and give you purpose and destiny. It is, in essence, the blueprint for your future.

God had a vision for the world when He created the garden of Eden. He planned for Adam and Eve to live a life of abundance, free from sin and all it embodies. He never intended them to experience death, shame, or loss. Even when creating humanity, God had a strong vision. Just as an architect takes time to construct an image of what he or she desires to build, God used His own image as a blueprint to fashion His man and woman. God is creative and purposeful, and we are too. The same way He builds is the same way we build. God's vision for humankind hasn't changed. His love for us still demands the best, but for His vision to come into fruition in your life, you must align your visions with His.

Ironically, the serpent too had a vision. He was empowered by the enemy, whose goal was to bring death and destruction into the lives of God's creation. Eve's problems began when she lost sight of God's vision and aligned herself with the enemy's. It is so easy, in a moment of temptation and frustration, to lose sight of the bigger picture if you don't hold tight to your godly vision. "Where there is no revelation, the people cast off restraint" (Prov. 29:18 NIV). A person with no vision has no future and will always return to his or her past.

Consider what happens when a convicted criminal escapes from prison. In order to locate the prisoner, the authorities return to his or her past: where this person used to go, who this person used to hang out with, and what this person's tendencies were. They do this because that criminal has no future; he or she only has the past to return to. About vision, Paul wrote:

> *Brethren, I count not myself to have apprehended: but this one thing I do, forgetting those things which are behind, and reaching forth unto those things which are before, I press toward the mark for the prize of the high calling of God in Christ Jesus* (Philippians 3:13–14).

Your vision should drive your focus. Eve could have avoided her fall if she had aligned her actions with God's vision rather than the temporary passions and temptations of her world. Focus isn't something that happens automatically; it is intentional and purposeful. Jesus died to redeem us from our past and restore us to the wonderful life that Adam and Eve forfeited, so don't allow subtle contradictions to limit your views and cause you to misstep.

REMOVE THE LIMITS

God declares over us, "For I know the plans I have for you, declares the Lord, plans to prosper you and not to harm you, plans to give you hope and a future" (Jer. 29:11 AMP). At times, what God sees is completely opposite to what we see. Sometimes obeying the voice of God seems downright crazy. God always sees the bigger picture, and He expects us to have confidence in Him even when it doesn't look the way we would like it to. The Bible says, "For as the heavens are higher than the earth, so are my ways higher than your ways, and my thoughts than your thoughts" (Isa. 55:9). God's motive concerning you is always love. That is a guarantee. He is not wishy-washy or up and down. He is not moody or double-minded, and He has not changed His mind about you. Even in times of extreme circumstances, God is still with you and for you, and if you trust Him, you will experience His best. As Peter said, "Therefore humble yourselves under the mighty hand of God, that He may exalt you in due time, casting all of your care upon Him, for He cares for you" (1 Pet. 5:6–7 NKJV).

When we live by our own thoughts, opinions, and conclusions, we place limits on God. Many times in my life, I have asked, "God, where are You?" while failing to realize that my own disobedience had limited His hand in my life. God's grace is abundant and always available when we are not operating in pride. The Bible says, "In all thy ways acknowledge him, and he shall direct thy paths" (Prov. 3:6). Let's be honest; sometimes it seems to make more sense to do it our own way, according to our limited knowledge and emotions. However, if you allow yourself to live by the standards of your feelings, you will always find yourself on the short end of life's stick.

Eve operated in pride when she chose her way over the Lord's way. Her actions communicated that she knew better than God concerning her life. How many times have we made that same mistake, prioritizing our opinions over the will of the Father? Pride is dangerous. It feels right in the moment, but it leaves great destruction in its wake.

> *Pride goeth before destruction, and an haughty spirit before a fall. Better is it to be of an humble spirit with the lowly, than to divide the spoil with the proud. He that handleth a matter wisely shall find good: and whoso trusteth in the LORD, happy is he* (Proverbs 16:18–20).

FORGOTTEN

What happens when you feel like God's way is just wrong? I remember on my thirtieth birthday feeling as if I needed to take matters into my own hands. I was crushed that I was still unmarried and that I didn't see any viable candidates. My love life felt like a desert, dry and unfruitful. All the Christian guys around me were taken or uninterested. I felt unwanted and forgotten. I had needs just like everyone else, but it seemed that my godly standards drained my prospects pool. It was hard and discouraging. With subtle serpent tactics, the enemy began parading ungodly men around me who were ready and willing. Too many times, I came close to forfeiting my crown and settling for a wolf in sheep's clothing. But thank God, I kept myself under the Word of God. Regularly hearing His Word is what allowed me to withstand the pressures that had come to steal my life. Regardless of what temptations you may be facing, the Word will do the same for you.

The Bible warns us:

> *Be sober, be vigilant; because your adversary the devil walks about like a roaring lion, seeking whom he may devour. Resist him, steadfast in the faith, knowing that the same sufferings are experienced by your brotherhood in the world* (1 Pet. 5:8–9 NKJV).

If there are those he can devour, then that means there are others that he cannot. No one wants to be devoured by Satan, but in order to avoid that, you must resist him. As I resisted the temptations to settle as a single woman, I didn't always feel good afterward. It looked as if I would be single forever. As a minister, I regularly travelled many states to preach the gospel, and each time I left a state without meeting "the one," I battled discouragement. Thank God, He had a bigger picture than what I was seeing. It took a few years for me to understand why the men in America didn't seem to see me. God had ordained a young British man living in England for me. The moment we met, he knew I was the one for him, even when I wasn't sure. He pursued me, fought for me, and even left his country for me. Several years later,

I am still happily married to him. I would have never imagined that my story would be an international love story, but I am so thankful. What's going on in your life may not make sense to you right now, but trust that God has something for you beyond what you can see. He is a rewarder of those who diligently seek Him when times are good and when times are bad (see Heb. 11:6). You can count on Him.

OBEDIENCE AND PROVISION

Many people disobey God in hopes of obtaining a provision of some sort. As a result, many prematurely jump into relationships, business dealings, and circumstances that end up bringing harm to them. Eve disobeyed God in order to know good and evil, thinking that would exalt her, when it ended up demoting her. There is a connection between obedience and provision. *Your present-day obedience sets up your future provision.* This principle also works in reverse: *Present disobedience derails future provisions.* Your obedience to God will always go farther than just that problem at hand. The story of the widow woman in 1 Kings 17 demonstrates this so clearly:

> *Then the word of the Lord came to him, saying, "Arise, go to Zarephath, who belongs to Sidon, and dwell there. See, I have commanded a widow there to provide for you"* (1 Kings 17:8–9 NKJV).

During this time, people were living under a great famine. Just prior to this, Elijah had said, "As the Lord God of Israel lives, before whom I stand, there shall not be dew nor rain these years, except at my word" (1 Kings 17:1 NKJV).

Despite the conditions of the land, God had been providing for Elijah supernaturally. Now God instructed him to find a particular widow, and she would take care of him. In today's culture, Elijah probably would have been cancelled for this. What was a man of God doing taking anything from a widow, especially during hard times? On the surface, that makes no sense. But God always has a plan:

> *So he arose and went to Zarephath. And when he came to the gate of the city, indeed a widow was there gathering sticks. And he called to her and said, "Please bring me a little water in a cup, that I may drink." And as she was going to get it, he called to her and said, "Please bring me a morsel of bread in your hand." So she said, "As the Lord your God lives, I do not have bread, only a handful of flour in a bin, and a little oil in a jar; and see, I am gathering a couple of sticks that I may go in and prepare it for myself and my son, that we may eat it, and die"* (1 Kings 17:10–12 NKJV).

From the previous verses, we know that the Lord had already spoken to the widow before Elijah arrived. I find it interesting that she responded well to his request for water but not to his request for food. Verse 12 reveals that not only was she a widow, but she barely had any food for herself or her child. She had plans to die, but God had other plans. I assume she had been crying out to God when He communicated this assignment to her. How strange that her request for provision would turn into an assignment to provide for someone else. It would seemingly make more sense for God to send Elijah to someone in a better situation, but God is not limited by what has happened or is happening in our lives. He wanted this woman to trust Him, despite how it looked, so that He could multiply the little that was in her hands.

> *And Elijah said to her, "Do not fear; go and do as you have said, but make me a small cake from it first, and bring it to me; and afterward make some for yourself and your son. For thus says the Lord God of Israel: 'The bin of flour shall not be used up, nor shall the jar of oil run dry, until the day the Lord sends rain on the earth'"* (1 Kings 17:13–14 NKJV).

Whenever it comes to obeying the Lord, especially in situations that don't make sense to the natural mind, you must deal with the fear that will arise to stop you. While God was trying to bless this woman, the enemy was most certainly trying to stop it. In dire situations like this, where you place your faith will determine your outcome. Whose report are you going to believe? Faith in God will always produce a breakthrough, but fear, which is faith in the lies of the wicked one, will rob you every time.

Ultimately, the widow made the right choice.

> *So she went away and did according to the word of Elijah; and she and he and her household ate for many days. The bin of flour was not used up, nor did the jar of oil run dry, according to the word of the Lord which He spoke by Elijah* (1 Kings 17:15–16 NKJV).

The widow's obedience brought provision for her house as well as for the prophet of God. The Bible doesn't specify the exact number of days they ate, but many is more than what her plans originally contained when she expected that she and her son would die. Her obedience prolonged her life and exploded her future, but the best part is that it didn't stop there.

UNEXPECTED TRAGEDY

Now it happened after these things that the son of the woman who owned the house became sick. And his sickness was so serious that there was no breath left in him. So she said to Elijah, "What have I to do with you, O man of God? Have you come to me to bring my sin to remembrance, and to kill my son?" And he said to her, "Give me your son." So, he took him out of her arms and carried him to the upper room where he was staying and laid him on his own bed. Then he cried out to the Lord and said, "O Lord my God, have You also brought tragedy on the widow with whom I lodge, by killing her son?" And he stretched himself out on the child three times, and cried out to the Lord and said, "O Lord my God, I pray, let this child's soul come back to him." Then the Lord heard the voice of Elijah; and the soul of the child came back to him, and he revived (1 Kings 17:17–22 NKJV).

The most beautiful part of this story is the prevision the Lord demonstrated when He chose the widow to care for

Elijah. He knew that tragedy was in her son's future, so He ordained for His prophet to be there to avert it. The widow, in her obedience, not only unlocked present-day provision but also a future provision that she did not even know she would need. If she had chosen not to obey the voice of the Lord, that prophet would not have been in her house to raise her dead son. Glory to God! We need not fear what the future may hold but instead can trust and obey the Lord, knowing that each step of obedience not only secures the present but also takes care of the future. We serve a mighty God!

ORDERED STEPS

The psalmist reassures us:

> *The steps of a good man are ordered by the Lord: and he delighteth in his way. Though he fall, he shall not be utterly cast down: for the Lord upholdeth him with his hand* (Psalm 37:23–24).

God knows everything you have been through, everything you are currently going through, and everything you will face in the future. Often, we are reactive. Once something happens, then we respond, but God is different. He is proactive. When you delight yourself in the Lord and allow Him to walk with you in your life, He will order your steps. *What does that mean?* It means that God is way out in front of anything that might come up against you. Just as He did for the widow, He already has made a way of escape for you (see 1 Cor. 10:13). We live in a fallen world, and yes, trials and tribulations will come, but you've already got a hook up. Even when you're not looking, God is equipping you and strengthening you to not only withstand the battle but to *win*! "Many are the afflictions of the righteous: but the Lord delivers him out of them all" (Ps. 34:19).

When my husband and I first married, we found a cozy little condo to rent. After a couple of years, we were actively trying for children, so we decided to take a leap and buy our first home together. Fortunately, our realtor was a friend of mine, and she went over and above to help us locate our dream family home. During our search, I found a home that I fell in love with, but my husband was a little bit skeptical about it, and as a result, it sold before we could make a bid. I was very disappointed. We started looking for a better home than that one, but it never popped up. Instead, we ended up buying a fixer in the neighborhood that I had grown up in. A couple years after we settled into our home, that dream home of mine popped right back up on the market. I couldn't believe it. I told my husband that this had to be God's will, as homes of that caliber rarely come back onto the market so quickly. However, my husband was again hesitant to proceed. He never had peace about that home. We missed out again. Until last year, I had a picture of that home on my vision board. I memorized the address and occasionally drove by it hoping it would again become available.

A few years later, God blessed us with a son. At the age of two, he was diagnosed with a condition that produced delays in his development. Quickly, I was thrust into a world that I didn't understand and hadn't even realized affected so many families: special needs. My siblings and I had only attended private Christian schools growing up. We never had to attend a public school, so I never planned on my son being educated in any other way. Once my son became of preschool age, we tried to enroll him in a couple of private Christian schools, only to be turned away. One of the schools outright said, "We are not accepting any special needs kids." As if the diagnosis itself wasn't enough, the realization that my son needed more than the Christian schools would offer was daunting to me. I had no concept of the public school system and the special education programs and therapies they offered, so when I was looking to buy a home, I ignored the school district associated with the home. As far as I knew, it didn't matter because the plan was for all our kids to attend Christian schools.

So here I was, believing God for the complete healing of my son while walking out the details day by day. I cried for days, maybe even weeks. *What was I supposed to do?* I had my concerns about public education, especially considering the woke society we live in today, but I didn't seem to have many options. I was afraid and frustrated. None of this fit my plan, but God had indeed ordered my steps long before my son was even born. It turns out the home we ended up purchasing was in a school district known for its premier special education programs. They had built a brand-new school right down the street from my home that opened the month before my son was to start school. The very first day, his special education teacher said to me, "Don't worry, Momma. I will love him like you love him while he is with me." I knew she was the one God had ordained to walk with my son through this season of his life. In addition to that, a few months in, I attended a parent evening in which we were introduced to the head of the special education program for our school district. When she stood up, I could hardly believe it! She was a friend I knew from church and with whom I used to sing in the choir. She had been quietly looking out for my son.

In addition to all of that, one day as I was going through some papers in my office, I came across the old listing ticket for the other house that I had so desperately wanted and that we missed twice. I looked it over and saw something I had never paid attention to before—the school district. This house was only a few minutes away yet was in a different school district, which I later learned does not have a good special education program. In fact, they're known to be one of the worst districts in the area for children with special needs. In that moment, it all became clear. God had shut the door to that other home, which had looked so good, because of His love for our family and my son. He knew things I did not know at the time, and He ordered our steps to our home, knowing it would be a blessing for our son. By faith, my son will not always need special education, but as we walk out his journey, we celebrate knowing that God has it all worked out. Here's a valuable lesson that I learned and would love to pass on to you: *Sometimes rejection is God's protection.*

The next time you feel discouraged or lose hope, remember these stories. It may seem like you are losing out, but with God there's always a bigger picture. Don't waste your time trying to figure it all out, but walk in peace, knowing He has you. In a world full of uncertainties, one thing is for sure: When you walk with God, everything will be alright.

Lesson Seven

Have a Grateful Heart

And the Lord God planted a garden eastward in Eden; and there he put the man whom he had formed. And out of the ground made the Lord God to grow every tree that is pleasant to the sight, and good for food; the tree of life also in the midst of the garden, and the tree of knowledge of good and evil (Genesis 2:8–9).

And the Lord God commanded the man, saying, Of every tree of the garden thou mayest freely eat: But of the tree of the knowledge of good and evil, thou shalt not eat of it: for in the day that thou eatest thereof thou shalt surely die (Genesis 2:16–17).

And the woman said unto the serpent, We may eat of the fruit of the trees of the garden: But of the fruit of the tree which is in the midst of the garden, God hath said, Ye shall not eat of it, neither shall ye touch it, lest ye die (Genesis 3:2–3).

When talking about the story of Adam and Eve, most often the only tree discussed is the forbidden tree of the knowledge of good and evil. That one tree became the focus in the conversation between the serpent and Eve, but the garden had many other trees as well. The Bible tells us that God created those other trees to be pleasant to the eyes and good for food. Those trees were in His will. Yet Eve forfeited an entire garden for one tree. The reason for her choice is also the root of many of our mess-ups: ingratitude. I believe the true poison in the garden was Eve's failure to be grateful for all God had provided for them. After all, He had freely given her access to all the other wonderful trees filled with fruit.

It's easy to emphasize the things we don't have rather than celebrate all that we do have. No matter what you may be going through, you can find something to be thankful for. You serve a faithful God whose love for you is abundant. He has blessed you beyond measure. But you will forget all His blessings if you focus on what you don't yet have. Thankfulness opens the door to God's blessings, while ingratitude opens your life to the thief. Psalm 100:4–5 tells us:

> *Enter his gates with thanksgiving and his courts with praise; give thanks to him and praise his name. For the Lord is good and his love endures forever; his faithfulness continues through all generations* (NIV).

The key to accessing the next level is learning to praise God on *every* level, during both the good and the bad. God's power thrives in an atmosphere of thanksgiving, so when you praise Him, you are never alone. Thanksgiving unlocks the power of God to work on your behalf, but a grateful heart is the prerequisite.

THE MIRACLE IN THE MESS

We all go through storms in our lives. If you've lived on this earth for a decent amount of time, you've probably experienced a shock wave or two that made you feel hopeless, like God had forgotten about you. In Mark 4, we read a story in which the disciples started to feel that way:

> *And the same day, when the even was come, he saith unto them, Let us pass over unto the other side. And when they had sent away the multitude, they took him even as he was in the ship. And there were also with him other little ships. And there arose a great storm of wind, and the waves beat into the ship, so that it was now full. And he was in the hinder part of the ship, asleep on a pillow: and they awake him, and say unto him, Master, carest thou not that we perish? And he arose, and rebuked the wind, and said unto the sea, Peace, be still. And the wind ceased, and there was a great calm* (Mark 4:35–39).

The disciples found themselves in a rough situation. This storm was so bad that if something didn't change quickly, they were surely going to drown. Or so they thought. The disciples were so focused on the storm and what it appeared to be doing that they completely missed the miracle in the mess. The waves had beat into the boat to the point that the boat was full of water (see Mark 4:37). A boat that is completely full of water is a *sunken boat!* If a boat is sinking, it means the water is filling up, but once it's completely full, the boat is sunken. The fact that the boat was full of water, yet still somehow floating, was a *miracle!* God's great grace was keeping them afloat. Yet they were so focused on the problem that they didn't notice the miracle. Instead, they accused Jesus, asking if He cared, when He was already holding them up. Wow!

If you reflect over your life, you will see many situations that should have been the end of you, but you are still here. People may have written you off, thinking you weren't worth much, but God held you up in that storm and got you to dry land. God is the ultimate businessman, and He does not waste space or time. The fact that you have life left in your body means God's grace is upon your life, and He is not done with you. Don't miss seeing His hand during the storm.

ATTITUDE OF GRATITUDE

Life happens to us all. Our ability to master the challenges and disappointments that arise is directly connected to the amount of victory we walk in. Life is not fair, but God is just. One of the greatest gifts you can give yourself is to learn to have an attitude of gratitude. It's so easy to murmur and complain when things get rough, but that never gets you out of the trouble. It just lengthens your time in it. The story of the children of Israel is a cautionary tale of what an ungrateful, complaining heart can do. Despite all God had done for them, the children of Israel were not thankful. Instead they complained.

> *And when the people complained, it displeased the Lord: and the Lord heard it; and his anger was kindled; and the fire of the Lord burnt among them and consumed them that were in the uttermost parts of the camp* (Numbers 11:1).

I used to think the children of Israel were nothing but a bunch of jerks. No matter how many miracles God did on their behalf, it just never seemed to be enough. God set them free from captivity in Egypt through a long series of miracles. When He brought them out of slavery, He did so with silver and gold. He also removed all sickness from them; not one person among them was sick. Not only did God free them and financially restore them with abundance from their enemies, but He also healed every man, woman, and child among them. Considering their many years of slavery, I imagine quite a few ailments were washed away. As the Israelites left Egypt, their enemies came after them, and God performed miracle after miracle, like parting the Red Sea, to keep them safe.

In addition to performing all of these miracles, God had also promised to take them to a land flowing with milk and honey. You would think they would adopt an attitude of extreme gratitude toward and confidence in God. But that was not the case. Instead, they murmured about the food and about Moses' wife. They built a golden altar to worship other gods. And by the time they arrived at the Promised Land, they didn't think it looked good, and they lost it.

They should have known that the same God who had been providing for them up to that point could handle any issues in the Promised Land, but their ungrateful attitude hampered their future and caused them to wish for the bonds of their past.

> *And all the congregation lifted their voice, and cried; and the people wept that night. And all the children of Israel murmured against Moses and against Aaron: and the whole congregation said unto them, Would God that we had died in the land of Egypt! or would God we had died in this wilderness! And wherefore hath the Lord brought us unto this land, to fall by the sword, that our wives and our children should be a prey? were it not better for us to return into Egypt? And they said one to another, Let us make a captain, and let us return into Egypt* (Numbers 14:1–4).

Like Eve, that generation disqualified themselves from receiving what God had set apart for them because of their ingratitude.

My Children of Israel Moment

In my life, I too had become like the children of Israel. I lost my attitude of gratitude. In my early 20s, I had found out that I might not be able to have children. Now that I was in my very late 30s and finally married, my chances were slim. My biological clock wasn't just ticking; it was on full alarm mode. So we started trying for a baby. It was a hard journey in which we lost two baby boys. This experience emotionally destroyed me to the point that I got tired of believing anything would change. Like the children of Israel, I forgot about all of the miracles I was already living in, like the fact that I was finally married. After all, my husband wasn't even American! God went all the way to a different country on a different continent to find my man, and He gave us a beautiful love story.

Then, in September of 2018, at the age of 40, I finally gave birth to our miracle baby, Lucas. I had believed for this baby for years. Because I was advanced in age, the doctors wanted to deliver my baby early. I overrode my peace and allowed them to try. It did not go well. After four long, hard days that ended in an unexpected C-section, I felt thoroughly disappointed. I had been believing for a supernatural childbirth like so many of the testimonies I had read about. *I wrote out my scriptures and confessions just like those other women had, so why wasn't my labor easy like theirs?* Some of my friends had seemingly pushed once and the baby just popped out, yet I had suffered through four days of pain. I was holding my miracle in my arms, yet I was mad about how it happened.

In addition, I was tired, and my self-satisfied attitude started to multiply. I started to get angry that my baby didn't look like me. Anytime someone mentioned that he looked like some other family member, I became more annoyed. To make matters worse, once I got home, I started getting offended with my husband because I had gone through all of that to have my baby, while he had done absolutely nothing. It just didn't seem fair. My hormones were going crazy, but it didn't have to be that way. Be careful when life gives you permission to be unthankful. Some well-meaning people told me it was normal for me to feel so miserable, but I soon learned the hard way that, as a child of God, I didn't have to accept that.

When the bills started to roll in, I murmured about that too. Our hospital bills were much higher than expected because of the failed four-day induction. I thought I would meet my insurance deductible, but to my surprise that didn't happen because the hospital put some of the charges in Lucas's name. Suddenly, I was looking at my baby like, "How is it that you have bills?" The disappointments just kept coming, and sure enough, I slipped into a depression. One night, a good friend came to sit with the baby so Lee and I could go out to dinner. Instead of enjoying it, I cried the entire time. I whined about everything that had gone wrong since before we were even married.

A Life Saved and an Attitude Changed

Then came November 1, 2018. Lucas was four weeks old. He had been having some comfort issues with his pajamas, so I decided to drive him to the store to purchase a different type. Normally, I would not have considered taking him out before he was six weeks old, but I felt like this was an emergency because I was tired of hearing him cry all night. We pulled into a packed parking lot outside of the baby store. I got out of the car, built up the stroller, locked the car seat into it, and began walking to the store. I was tired, and I hoped the new baby pajamas might enable me to get a better night's sleep. We hadn't even made it to the intersection of the lot when, out of nowhere, an SUV plowed into me and my four-week-old baby as we were walking. I heard a loud bang as the SUV hit the stroller and then a deafening silence. Just minutes before I was grumpy and looking for anything to silence my baby so I could sleep. Now his cry was the only thing I wanted to hear.

We ended up in the trauma room at our local hospital. I will never forget how stupid I felt as I watched the doctors work on my son. I had been complaining about whether he looked like me, his birth story, how tired I was, and how old I was. But in that moment, watching the trauma doctors take him out of that car seat to check him out, I realized how trivial all of that was. Here was this amazing gift that I had prayed, fought, and longed for, but instead of being thankful, I had been griping and complaining about every little thing. Now I could not find enough *thank yous* in the world to describe how happy I was that he was alive!

Four or five medical personnel were checking him out at the same time. Some were working his legs, others his arms, others his reflexes in hopes of explaining his loud cries. Turned out he just wanted a bottle. As soon as they gave him one, he quieted down. Praise God! Not only had God spared our lives, but He had given me a new perspective that changed my life.

I realized just how fast and unfair Satan is, coming after a four-week-old baby. I believe Satan felt he had the right to come in and take that precious gift away from me, but by the grace and mercy of God, he failed. A few days later, another realization came to light. God had been involved long before that dark night. After the accident, we had to scrap the car seat as it was damaged, but the stroller was a different story. A family friend had gifted a very high-end titanium stroller to us. It was very tall and built in such a way that it placed the baby up very high. I would not have spent the money for that stroller, but God placed it on our friend's heart months before. That person had no idea what would happen, but God knew what was coming, and He had already set us up. That stroller took the hit from the SUV and didn't even sustain a scratch. I believe the high placement of the baby, as well as the strength of the stroller, helped Lucas avoid injury.

Amazingly, the moment I changed my heart and adopted an attitude of gratitude, the depression left. My life improved drastically even though many of the circumstances were still the same. What had changed was me. Sure, I was still tired, and I had some recovering to do after the accident, but I was thankful. What used to drive me crazy now caused me joy! I would rather have a screaming baby keeping me up in the promised land than be back in Egypt praying for God to open my womb. Fear tried to grip me for several months, but I kept our testimony in the forefront of my mind. I did not have to fear parking lots or SUVs because the same God who blessed me with my husband, healed me from cancer, gave me my baby boy, and protected our lives is the same God who is walking with me day in and day out. He's not reactive; He's proactive.

That same God loves you, and if you take a moment to reflect, you will see His miraculous hand all throughout your life. You're still here, and that's something to celebrate.

I've learned the secret to a happy life. It's not flawless relationships or perfect circumstances; it's a grateful heart.

HAPPY IN YOUR OWN SKIN

Are you happy in your own skin, or do you wish for someone else's? Clearly, Eve's lack of contentment pushed her out of God's place for her in the garden, and if we are not careful, we can suffer the same fate. It's so easy to want what you don't have or become what I like to call a "professional wisher." At one time, that phrase described me, because I spent so much of my time wishing I had what others had—from their talents to their hair to their body type. God moves through people. God uses people, but to be used by Him, you must get past the insecurities and lies from Satan that are holding you back from what God has ordained for you to do. Where God wants you to be is where you will find your blessing, your provision, and your overflow. In addition, other people will be blessed by what God can do through you.

The Bible tells us the key to happiness: "Happy is the man that finds wisdom, and the man that getteth understanding" (Prov. 3:13). Notice that happiness doesn't come from having the best car, the nicest purse, the slimmest body, or the biggest house. Instead, happiness comes from gaining wisdom and understanding from God, not from somebody else's opinion. You don't have to have the perfect body to do something great for God. The fact that the lady down the aisle has a better job than yours and makes more money does not mean she is happier than you. You won't gain anything in your life by comparing yourself to other people. The Bible says, "But godliness with contentment is great gain" (1 Tim. 6:6).

God wants to take you to higher levels and use you mightily, but it starts with changing your focus from meditating on what you feel you're missing to acknowledging and celebrating what He has given you. Whether you see it or not, God has given you so much, so be happy in your own skin. It is time to be at peace with yourself and what God has called you to do with the abilities, gifts, and graces He has placed on your life. If you don't get that settled, you will never have the impact He has ordained for you.

The apostle Paul said, "For by grace are ye saved through faith; and that not of yourselves: it is the gift of God" (Eph. 2:8). The grace that saved you wasn't because you had it all together but because God chose to gift it to you. You cannot do anything apart from God. Without God's grace, you wouldn't even have the ability to comprehend this book. The mere fact that you woke up this morning is a manifestation of His grace on your life. Here's what's wonderful about this verse: Because you didn't earn grace and you didn't work it up, you also don't have to worry about trying to work it up for the rest of your life. That takes the pressure off, because that gift is in you. You should always have something in your life that you can't explain, because you have God on the inside. He's doing in you what you cannot do by yourself. That's another reason why you can be happy in your own skin.

Recently, I was on social media and came across a comment on one of my Instagram reels where I was preaching about the goodness of God. This person must have been dealing with great disappointment, because he commented that he had been crying out to Jesus for years, and He was nowhere to be found. My heart went out to this individual because it was clear, like so many today, that he had failed to recognize God's presence in his day-to-day life. I replied that God's hand was evident in the mere fact that he was alive and able to comment. I told him that there are many people in a grave who would willingly trade places with him, despite whatever issues he is battling. I also pointed out that the reel itself was a result of God reaching out to him to remind him how loved he is. It is so easy to overlook God's hand in our lives when we are hurt and discouraged, but His gift to us was and is abundant, no matter what challenges may arise.

THE KEY

The author of Hebrews offers us the key to this perspective shift: "By him therefore let us offer the sacrifice of praise to God continually, that is, the fruit of our lips giving thanks to his name" (Heb. 13:15). Thankfulness is the key to being at peace with yourself despite your flaws, issues, and imperfections. Thanksgiving involves remembering and valuing. It changes your focus away from what you feel is missing to what you do have in your hands. You may not be where you want to be, but be thankful that it's not over and God is not done with you. Never despise small beginnings, and do not belittle what God has done in you so far.

When I was in my early 20s and had just begun preaching, I found myself in an intimidating situation. I had only preached publicly a handful of times at my church in some of the smaller services. I was just learning to be comfortable preaching, and I had not yet taken on a main service. Every year, our church held our annual convention in which the best of the best were invited to speak. It was always an anointed time. The church was always packed, and people looked forward to the special impartations from seasoned special guest ministers who travelled from across the country to impart an on-time word.

It was a Friday night, and a world-renowned minister had just preached the house down! The service was amazing, and God had indeed moved mightily. My mother, a wonderful minister herself, had been scheduled for the next session, which was Saturday morning. However, she fell ill late Friday night. It was almost midnight when my father approached me to tell me that I was to preach in her stead. I'm sorry to say that I completely freaked out. I cried and cried and cried. No one wanted to hear from a 21-year-old preacher, especially not after all the superstar preachers who had previously ministered. My emotions were all over the place. I went from being angry with my father to feeling sorry for myself to feeling afraid that I would fall on my face. I didn't get much sleep that night; in fact, I didn't even try. As I lay awake staring at an empty page that was to be my message, the Lord dropped a lesson in my heart that still serves me to this day.

That night, I prayed harder than I ever had, asking the Lord to help me rise to the occasion that I felt so unqualified for. He instructed me to write out what I had to be thankful for. I thought, *Are you serious? How is this supposed to help me get through this sermon?* But as I began my list, the Holy Spirit prompted me to be purposeful and specific in my gratitude. I started off with the more obvious things to be thankful for, but the deeper I got the more I felt the power of God rising on the inside of me. I began to thank Him for even the most trivial things, like my teeth, nostrils, skin, freckles, ear lobes, arms, legs, fingers, fingernails, eyes, and so on. I moved on to thanking God for the clothes and shoes I would wear, for the comb and brush I had to prepare my hair. I thanked Him for my car and the gas in it, for pen and paper and the ability to write, think, read, eat, and drink. I thanked Him for the pillows and sheets on my bed, the carpet on my floor and paint on my walls. I thanked Him for my balance that allowed me to walk and the vocal cords that allowed me to speak. I ran out of paper before I ran out of things to be thankful for. Let me tell you, that night I learned a striking lesson: There is power in *specific* thanksgiving. No matter how big or intimidating the circumstance around you may be, it loses power when you start to recognize how much God has already done for you!

The next morning, I not only ministered the Word of God with power, but it was one of the best messages I have ever preached, and I came away with an invaluable lesson. Eve may have felt like she was missing something when the serpent challenged her to disobey God, but imagine how quickly the serpent would have been quieted if she had responded by openly praising God for Adam, the animals, the trees, the fruit, the rivers, the herbs, the oceans, and so forth. That serpent wouldn't have known what hit him.

Likewise, let us not just live a life of gratitude but of specific thanksgiving. No mountain is too big to overcome for a woman with a grateful heart.

Lesson Eight

Stay Focused

And when the woman saw that the tree was good for food, and that it was pleasant to the eye, and a tree to be desired to make wise, she took of the fruit thereof, and did eat, and gave also unto her husband with her; and he did eat (Genesis 3:6).

When I was younger, my parents would often take my siblings and me to the circus. I loved seeing all the animals perform, but I was most in awe of the lion tamer. I often held my breath as I watched the huge beast with large teeth and gigantic paws be controlled with a whip and a stool. How the tamer escaped with his life was beyond me, but it certainly kept me entertained. Not until I was older did I learn about the strategy behind taming such a powerful animal. I was shocked to learn that much of it comes down to the legs on the stool. When the tamer needs to exercise dominion over the beast, he holds up a chair with multiple legs. The lion, seeing each leg, tries to focus on all of them at the same time and is, thus, rendered powerless. So the weaker lion tamer could dominate the much stronger lion simply because the lion's focus was scattered.

There's a huge lesson in that: It all comes down to focus.

THE IMPORTANCE OF A GOOD FOCUS

We see this same principle in action with Eve. As we have previously discussed, she was wonderfully made in the image and likeness of God, and God gave her dominion over all the animals, including the serpent (see Gen. 1:26). However, just like the lion tamer, the serpent used a distraction to nullify Eve's power. So many times, we give away our position when we allow distractions to come in and choke our purpose. The truth is, Adam and Eve were graced to do plenty of other things. In addition to the blessings they had received in the garden, God also gave them assignments in stewarding the garden. For example, in Genesis 2:15, God told them to dress the garden and keep it. Considering the size of the garden, that was a full-time job. Pondering the suggestions of the enemy provided no benefit to Eve; it was just a distraction.

Adam and Eve's blessings were found in God's will, not in Satan's contradictions. They found provision in walking out the purpose God had placed on their lives. The serpent's assertions about the tree of the knowledge of good and evil was nothing but an attempt to steal their focus. It had no value in relation to the quality of their lives, gifts, and authority in the garden. However, because Eve allowed her focus to be shifted, she inadvertently started down the path that eventually led to destruction. Clearly, good focus is powerful.

A FIGHT TO FOCUS

Many things in your life are competing for your focus. The increase in technology has been a blessing in many ways, but it has also increased the number of distractions and diversions that regularly present themselves. You can be in your home minding your own business, but that little rectangular phone that fits in your hand can push drama and distraction right into your space. How do you stay focused when so many things vie for your attention? It starts with taking responsibility for your focus.

Here's a valuable truth that will serve you well: You are always in control of your focus. You may not have any control over what's going on around you, but you do have complete control over what you decide to zero-in on. Jesus' counsel about worry makes that clear:

> *Give your entire attention to what God is doing right now, and don't get worked up about what may or may not happen tomorrow. God will help you deal with whatever hard things come up when the time comes* (Matthew 6:34 MSG).

Trials and tribulations often show up in our lives right before great triumphs. In a previous chapter, we discussed the storm Jesus and the disciples encountered and how the disciples were living in a miracle even during the storm (see Mark 4:25–41). But we can glean more from that story. One day, while I was studying that passage, the Lord asked me this question, "What did the storm come to stop?" I had never thought about it like that. I had taught that passage so many times, but I had always stopped at the end of chapter 4. So I sat down and read Mark 5:1–20. Sure enough, after Jesus and the disciples made it through the storm and onto land, they encountered a previously uncurable demon-possessed man. It was so bad that even chains and ropes couldn't hold him down. Jesus set that man free! After that, we read about the miracles of Jesus raising Jairus's daughter from the dead and healing the woman with the issue of blood. I finally saw it! That storm was a distraction sent to stop the miraculous power of God. It didn't work in the life of Jesus, and it doesn't have to work in your life either. Jesus wasn't distracted by the storm. Instead, He commanded it to be still:

> *And he was in the hinder part of the ship, asleep on a pillow: and they awake him, and say unto him, Master, carest thou not that we perish? And he arose, and rebuked the wind, and said unto the sea, Peace, be still. And the wind ceased, and there was a great calm. And he said unto them, Why are ye so fearful? how is it that ye have no faith?* (Mark 4:38–40).

The fact that Jesus was sleeping in the back of the boat during that storm is a powerful statement. Jesus didn't allow Himself to get all worked up in that distraction. He didn't allow fear and worry to grip Him. You may be asking, "How could He sleep when all hell was breaking loose around them?" It's simple: the Word of the Lord had already been spoken. Before they set out for their trip, Jesus had said, "Let us pass over unto the other side" (Mark 4:35). Jesus spoke the word and believed what He had spoken. They would pass over to the other side. In fact, they had work to do on the other side. There was enough power in those words—"Let us pass over unto the other side"—to deal with anything that would or could possibly arise.

Thus, when everyone else was freaking out at the storm, Jesus was preparing for the triumphs on the other side. He knew great victories were waiting beyond the distraction, so He rested His body instead of stressing it out. He rested so He could walk out the fullness of those victories. Some of us are so tired, not because we can't handle life, but because of how we choose to respond to distractions.

The Word that you take into your heart before the storm will determine how you ride through it. You will have a hard time focusing on something you do not know. When you're going through, you must know the Word of the Lord concerning your situation, and you must choose to focus on that.

When I was diagnosed with cancer, thank God I was able to pull out the Bible and see God's will concerning my body and my life. First Peter 2:24 told me that by Jesus' stripes I was already healed, so I had to choose to make that my focus as I walked through the battle. The gospel is called the good news because God's Word is full of truth that contradicts the lies of the enemy. A sick person doesn't have to stay sick; that's good news. A depressed person doesn't have to stay depressed; that's good news. A poor person doesn't have to stay broke; that's good news.

The key is maintaining our focus on the truth of God's Word and refusing the lies of distraction. As the apostle Paul wrote:

> *Finally, brethren, whatsoever things are true, whatsoever things are honest, whatsoever things are just, whatsoever things are pure, whatsoever things are lovely, whatsoever things are of good report; if there be any virtue, and if there be any praise, think on these things* (Philippians 4:8).

What you focus on is what you will manifest. Eve focused on the lies of the enemy. She entertained them in her thought life, and those lies took hold of her life. Let's do better. Make a quality decision today to not only keep the truth of God's Word in the forefront of your mind but also to refuse to allow anything to distract you from all that God has given. A distraction always presents itself before a breakthrough. Don't let the distraction scare you. Grab hold of the breakthrough and allow the Lord to see you through. We need faith and courage to walk through the valley of the shadow of death, but make no mistake about it, it's a walk *through*. Jesus has already paid the price for every victory, blessing, and restoration that we will ever need. Focus on that and accept nothing less.

THE WALK-THROUGH

When you are going through tough times, it is important not only to recognize God's provisions but also to see the part you must play to stay focused and walk out your victory.

Psalm 23 is one of my favorite passages that I meditate on, especially during challenging times.

> *The Lord is my Shepherd [to feed, to guide and to shield me], I shall not want. He lets me lie down in green pastures; He leads me beside the still and quiet waters. He refreshes and restores my soul (life); He leads me in the paths of righteousness for His name's sake. Even though I walk through the [sunless] valley of the shadow of death, I fear no evil, for You are with me; Your rod [to protect] and Your staff [to guide], they comfort and console me. You prepare a table before me in the presence of my enemies. You have anointed and refreshed my head with oil; my cup overflows. Surely good-ness and mercy and unfailing love shall follow me all the days of my life, and I shall dwell forever [throughout all my days] in the house and in the presence of the Lord* (Psalm 23 AMP).

If you find yourself walking through the valley of the shadow of death, let me encourage you to start with verse 5. The mere fact that God is preparing a table for you means that He has confidence that you will overcome whatever issues are trying to hold you back. The God who knows all things—every thought, every flaw, and every detail—expects you to come through this storm, so don't lose hope. Keep your mind set on this truth: With God, you *will overcome!* Despite the number of weapons, issues, or even people that may form against you, with God you are a majority, an all-star team. You and God are co-laborers in your victory. God will always be faithful to perform His part, but you must also do your part, so stay focused and walk it out.

God is ever present even in the darkest moments of our lives. This psalm reveals that He is our shepherd. He leads, guides, restores, and is with us. He comforts and protects with His rod and staff. He prepares our future and anoints and covers us with His overflowing power. He assigns goodness and mercy to be our travel buddies everywhere we go and invites us to be with Him forever. What a wonderful God we serve.

Likewise, this psalm also provides wisdom about the part we must play in our own victories. In every challenge, you have an opportunity to be the prophet of your own life. The very words you speak are what you are giving power to in your situation. Notice that David didn't begin this psalm talking about the problem, but instead he made a proclamation: *I shall not lack!* His focus wasn't on the problem, but he was declaring the end from the beginning. If you want to experience the restorative power of God, do yourself a favor and make a quality decision to release your faith in God's ability to take the wrongs and make them right in your life. He is a good Father.

Verse 4 highlights the process of a victorious life: *I will walk through!* It's so easy to sit down and get stuck wallowing in self-pity and fear, but keep stepping. Manifestations don't always happen overnight. That's no excuse to sit down and give up. God never wastes a battle, and He will use what Satan meant to destroy you to bring you out. I love the story of David and Goliath in the Old Testament. The sword that was made and fashioned for the champion Goliath is the very sword that David used to cut off Goliath's head (see 1 Sam. 17:51). Don't allow the weapons that are coming against you make you turn back; keep pushing, knowing that it will all turn out for your good.

Every successful battle requires precision: *I will not fear!* In order to have good precision you must have a laser focus. After all, miracles do happen even in the valley. A shadow may look scary, but remember it only exists because light is also present. Don't allow fear to dampen your spirit. God has filled you with His light, so turn it up. That bright light chases away all of the shadows.

Last, let me encourage you in the fight to recognize the purpose: *I will dwell!* Verse 6 highlights that this love is an everlasting love; it's not temporary. God wants to dwell with you forever, but that means you must show up and keep showing up. It's always too soon to quit. God has made a place for you, so don't let that preparation and sacrifice go to waste by being a no-show. Keep your head up and your focus on Jesus. He will always see you through.

Keep It Simple

And the woman said unto the serpent, We may eat of the fruit of the trees of the garden: But of the fruit of the tree which is in the midst of the garden, God hath said, Ye shall not eat of it, neither shall ye touch it, lest ye die. And the serpent said unto the woman, Ye shall not surely die: For God doth know that in the day ye eat thereof, then your eyes shall be opened, and ye shall be as gods, knowing good and evil. And when the woman saw that the tree was good for food, and that it was pleasant to the eyes, and a tree to be desired to make one wise, she took of the fruit thereof, and did eat, and gave also unto her husband with her; and he did eat (Genesis 3:2–6).

So many things in this life can be very complicated, which contributes to much of the stress we face. At times, life can feel overwhelming. But one reality is as simple as it gets: His name is Jesus Christ. In all the circumstances and pressures we attempt to manage daily, following Jesus is the only way to victory. Obedience is better than sacrifice.

FORBIDDEN THOUGHTS

In Genesis 3, it's clear that the serpent's aim was to change the way Eve *thought* about the forbidden fruit. He understood what so many fail to realize even today: Thoughts are the blueprints upon which actions follow. As the Bible says:

> *For those who live according to the flesh set their minds on the things of the flesh, but those who live according to the Spirit, the things of the Spirit. For to be carnally minded is death, but to be spiritually minded is life and peace* (Romans 8:5–6 NKJV).

In Genesis 3:6, Satan's plan fell into place the moment Eve decided to take a second glance at the fruit. She went from being resolute about what God had said in verse 2 to taking another look in verse 6. I can imagine the kind of questions that probably went through her head: *What if the serpent is right? What if it is better to know good and evil than to not know? Could God have been exaggerating about the death part? Was He just using a scare tactic?* Sure, life was already great, but maybe it would be better if she just took a small bite. Fruit that looked that good couldn't really be bad. So many thoughts, and so many questions—all so complicated, yet missing the simple truth. If God said it, you can take it to the bank. Sure, the serpent wove a tale and presented it masterfully, but Eve would have saved herself a world of trouble if she had kept it simple and said, "I believe God."

The apostle Paul warned the church of Corinth about this very issue when he wrote, "But I fear, lest by any means, as the serpent beguiled Eve through his subtilty, so your minds should be corrupted from the simplicity that is in Christ" (2 Cor. 11:3). The simplicity found in Christ is the remedy to the subtle deceptions of the enemy.

So many women still fall victim to this tactic of the devil. His plan today hasn't changed from that fateful day in Eden. He's still aiming to change the way you think about sin, because he hates you. The Bible calls him a thief whose motives are to steal, kill, and destroy (see John 10:10), and he uses trickery and foolish reasonings to entice us to sin. This may not be popular to say today, but it is the truth: The wages of sin are death, just as they were in the garden, and Satan will do anything to get you not only caught up in it but also good and comfortable in it. He would love to see the destruction that sin brings become your normal. Jesus warned, "The thief cometh not, but for to steal, and to kill, and to destroy: I am come that they might have life, and that they might have it more abundantly" (John 10:10).

In a world of chaos filled with noise from social media, cancel culture, ungodly opinions, and foolish debates from every side, one standard will never lead you astray. This standard is clear and simple: *Does what I am seeing, hearing, or considering line up with the Word of God?* If it does, it is good. If it doesn't, don't even entertain it. Other people may not understand. They may even attempt to fight you on it. However, your security and peace are not found in the opinions of others but simply in the will of the Lord. His love for you is abundant, and His motives concerning you are the same as they were for Eve in the garden—to give you a life of peace, joy, and abundance.

For this reason, we must refuse to listen to the noise and keep our focus on Jesus. As 2 Corinthians 10:4–5 says, this is how we get our victory:

> *For the weapons of our warfare are not physical [weapons of flesh and blood], but they are mighty before God for the overthrow and destruction of strongholds, [Inasmuch as we] refute arguments and theories and reasonings and every proud and lofty thing that sets itself up against the [true] knowledge of God; and we lead every thought and purpose away captive into the obedience of Christ (the Messiah, the Anointed One)* (AMPC).

STOP TRYING TO FIGURE IT OUT

> *Therefore I say to you, do not worry about your life, what you will eat or what you will drink; nor about your body, what you will put on. Is not life more than food and the body more than clothing? Look at the birds of the air, for they neither sow nor reap nor gather into barns; yet your heavenly Father feeds them. Are you not of more value than they? Which of you by worrying can add one cubit to his stature?* (Matthew 6:24–27 NKJV).

One way to shoot yourself in the foot and rob your peace is to spend your life trying to figure everything out. How is this going to happen? How is God going to get it done? What about what's going on over there? What's going to happen when I get older? Living a life of worry is complicated and stressful, and it is not the will of God. I still struggle with worry in my life from time to time. Women tend to be big worriers. Sometimes we feel that the more we stress and worry, the more caring we are being. However, worrying doesn't add to your life; it subtracts. God is very clear to remind us to stop worrying about every little detail:

> *So why do you worry about clothing? Consider the lilies of the field, how they grow: they neither toil nor spin; and yet I say to you that even Solomon in all his glory was not arrayed like one of these. Now if God so clothes the grass of the field, which today is, and tomorrow is thrown into the oven, will He not much more clothe you, O you of little faith?* (Matthew 6:28–30 NKJV).

Worrying reveals a lack of faith. When our confidence in God is low, fear inevitably enters in and chokes out our faith. However, God is admonishing us here to show that we can trust in Him. Lilies are one of the most beautiful flowers ever created, and they can self-pollinate, which means they are self-sufficient. They didn't work for that; they didn't sweat for that. God freely designed them that way. So why do you think He hasn't taken care of the details in your life?

Therefore do not worry, saying, "What shall we eat?" or "What shall we drink?" or "What shall we wear?" For after all these things the Gentiles seek. For your heavenly Father knows that you need all these things. But seek first the kingdom of God and His righteousness, and all these things shall be added to you. Therefore do not worry about tomorrow, for tomorrow will worry about its own things. Sufficient for the day is its own trouble (Matthew 6:31–34 NKJV).

It's as simple as that. The world is complex; it offers us plenty of things to worry about. But when you focus on walking with God, everything else will be taken care of. God made it so simple. God has your back, and when you trust Him, He will take care of your yesterdays, todays, and tomorrows.

WHEN ANXIETY STRIKES

Anxiety is a real problem for many people. Satan uses it to create secret warfare in the minds of many by introducing the worry about what *might* happen. Anxiety is terrorism of the mind, because when people live in anxiety, they are constantly living under the *threat* of what could happen. Anxiety comes to steal your peace. Without it, you cannot enjoy the life Jesus has given you. Even good things can become a burden in anxiety, because instead of being able to enjoy them, the fear of losing them overtakes us. Many people are imprisoned by things that have not even happened. The "what if" threat steals their joy and robs them of their future. Anxiety is a prison with many inmates, but the Word of God shows us how to break out of that jail cell.

> *Do not be anxious or worried about anything, but in everything [every circumstance and situation] by prayer and petition with thanksgiving, continue to make your [specific] requests known to God. And the peace of God [that peace which reassures the heart, that peace] which transcends all understanding, [that peace which] stands guard over your hearts and your minds in Christ Jesus [is yours]* (Philippians 4:6–7 AMP).

In this passage, we see three weapons to use against anxiety. The first is prayer. Often, when we are facing issues, we tend to talk to everyone except God. But there is power in prayer. If my son is having an issue, I want him to come running to me. I want him to trust me with his heart and allow me to help him. Likewise, prayer is communication with God. He wants you to spend time with Him, especially when you are struggling. When you're really facing the fire, pray through the trouble. The greater the pressure, the more you should pray. Supernatural strength comes as a result of spending time with God.

The second weapon is petition of the Lord. Make your request known to Him. You will find humility in turning your issues over to Him and trusting Him to handle them. God is interested in the details of your life, so get specific. When you release your faith in His ability to help you, you open the doors for His power to move on your behalf.

The third weapon is thanksgiving. When you stand right in the middle of your storm and praise God, no devil in hell will be able to triumph over you. Satan wants you miserable and afraid, but instead, take on an attitude of gratitude.

Those three weapons will release the peace of God back into your life. This isn't just any peace. This peace isn't subject to what's going on, but it is a Holy Ghost reaction to the storms of life. Natural peace exists when we don't have any battles, but the peace of God goes above any circumstance and beyond anything we can understand. We see a real-life example of this kind of peace in action when Jesus and the disciples were caught in a ferocious storm in Mark 4. Everything around them was saying they would die; the boat was filled with water and being tossed like a wet rag. The disciples were frantic and afraid, which is a normal response, but Jesus was operating in a higher realm. He was asleep in the middle of that storm, and then He calmed the storm with His faith (see Mark 4:35–41).

We have the same ability that Jesus demonstrated on that boat. You don't have to lose sleep, stress out, and be anxious. When you operate in the peace of God, especially in the dangerous times we live in today, you are walking in God's supernatural power. Anxiety is no match for God's peace. No matter how tough things get or how many attacks form against you, don't sweat it. Keep it simple, turn it over to God, and rest in His everlasting peace.

For the mountains shall depart, and the hills be removed; but my kindness shall not depart from thee, neither shall the covenant of peace be removed, saith the Lord that hath mercy on thee (Isaiah 54:10).

THE LITTLE THINGS

So many of us are looking for the next *big thing* in our lives. If you are like me, and you are believing God for some big manifestations, then let me invite you to focus on the little things in your life. After all, when we desire big changes for our lives, figuring out what big steps to take can become overwhelming. In fact, a lot of people get intimidated by that thought and never try at all. Jesus offers us a different way in this parable of the Kingdom:

> *Another parable put he forth unto them, saying, The kingdom of heaven is like to a grain of mustard seed, which a man took, and sowed in his field: Which indeed is the least of all seeds: but when it is grown, it is the greatest among herbs, and becometh a tree, so that the birds of the air come and lodge in the branches thereof* (Matthew 13:31–32).

Jesus was discussing the Kingdom of Heaven, which I dare say is big, yet He compared it to a little seed that, given time, grows to be larger than anything we can imagine. A lot of battles are lost when we only want to focus on the big things that everyone can see while ignoring those smaller day-to-day decisions that shape our very future. This is what Solomon meant when he wrote, "Take us the foxes, the little foxes, that spoil the vines: for our vines have tender grapes" (Song 2:15).

Too many people have been taken down not by the big things but by the small things that were left unchecked and thus grew into monsters that produced havoc in their lives. Adam and Eve didn't succumb to a huge thing but merely to a piece of fruit. Samson wasn't defeated by a large army but by his lust for a strange woman. David's troubles began with an unchecked peek at a naked lady bathing. Judas betrayed Jesus and started on the path toward suicide as a result of his misplaced love of money—the equivalent of 20 dollars today. Small things neglected will lead to big trouble every time.

Life is made up of small things, so we should pay attention to them. We all desire great things in our lives, but even the biggest harvests start with a small seed. "While the earth remaineth, seedtime and harvest, and cold and heat, and summer and winter, and day and night shall not cease" (Gen. 8:22). The law of seedtime and harvest is still in effect today and will work for those who put it into practice in their lives. If you want to live in the fullness of what God has for you, learn to be faithful and excellent in the little things, day by day. It may seem small and insignificant, but how you handle the small things is exactly how you will handle the big ones. God gave Adam and Eve dominion over the entire garden. In time, they could have expanded their influence beyond that, because they carried the nature of God on the inside of them. However, because they failed to be faithful over one tree, they never got to experience the fullness of what God created them for.

Jesus demonstrates this in Matthew 25 with the parable of the talents. The servants who worked well with what they had received more from their lord. He said to them, "Well done, thou good and faithful servant: thou hast been faithful over a few things, I will make thee ruler over many things: enter thou into the joy of thy Lord" (Matt. 25:21).

Neglected Littles

People tend to neglect the little things because they seem mundane and unimportant, and their results are often invisible for a time. It's like that mustard seed. When it is planted, it looks like nothing for a great many days. But that seed must be watered and nurtured long before it ever breaks out of the ground on its journey to greatness. The story of David and Goliath demonstrates this so well (see 1 Sam. 17:17–58). While David is famous for defeating the giant known as Goliath, we would be amiss to ignore the little steps he took to get to that field of victory.

David only arrived at the battle because of his obedience to his father's command to take food to his brothers. He could have just as easily chosen not to obey. However, not only did David honor his father's wishes, but he also approached them in excellence. He rose early and made provisions for his sheep in order to carry out that mission (see 1 Sam. 17:20). What if David had been late or had waited until the last minute to find someone to watch his sheep? He might have missed all the action. Instead, he fulfilled this seemingly minor task with excellence.

Then, when he heard Goliath's challenge, he responded with great courage. It was not by accident that such a young boy found the courage to take on a huge giant. David explained the process that prepared him to be brave in that moment:

> *Thy servant slew both the lion and the bear: and this uncircumcised Philistine shall be as one of them, seeing he hath defied the armies of the living God. David said moreover, The Lord that delivered me out of the paw of the lion, and out of the paw of the bear, he will deliver me out of the hand of this Philistine. And Saul said unto David, Go, and the Lord be with thee* (1 Samuel 17:36–37).

David was a keeper of sheep. He spent every day taking care of them and protecting them. It was not an exciting or impressive job. In fact, David's brothers seemed to look down on him for his role as a shepherd. But the lessons he learned as a lowly shepherd, the problems he had to work through, the dangers he had to overcome to protect his sheep, built his knowledge of and confidence in God. That is what allowed him to defeat the champion giant. If David had neglected the lessons of his early shepherding days, surely he never would have become a king. We would all do well to heed the advice of Zechariah: "Do not despise these small beginnings..." (Zech. 4:10a NLT).

In the Right Hands

Your little can become extremely big in the hands of God. The Bible says the steps of the righteous are ordained by the Lord (see Ps. 37:23). It doesn't say *leaps* but *steps*. What may seem insignificant and small to others can, in the right hands, be more than enough. The Bible tells a story of a little boy with a two-piece fish dinner. His five loaves and two fish seemed insignificant when aiming to feed thousands. It wasn't enough in his own hands, but the miracle happened when he placed what he had in the hands of Jesus:

> *There is a lad here, which hath five barley loaves, and two small fishes: but what are they among so many? And Jesus said, Make the men sit down. Now there was much grass in the place. So the men sat down, in number about five thousand. And Jesus took the loaves; and when he had given thanks, he distributed to the disciples, and the disciples to them that were set down; and likewise of the fishes as much as they would. When they were filled, he said unto his disciples, Gather up the fragments that remain, that nothing be lost. Therefore they gathered them together, and filled twelve baskets with the fragments of the five barley loaves, which remained over and above unto them that had eaten* (John 6:9–13).

Perhaps you have found yourself in sabotaging situations simply because you have failed to realize just how big what you have really is. I doubt that young lad woke up that day thinking his little lunch would end up feeding thousands with leftovers. Likewise, you may feel miniscule and insignificant, but in the arms of God, you have and are more than enough. You aren't too little for this fight!

Maybe you're just hidden, set aside for the appointed time that God has destined for you. Don't underestimate the days of preparation in your life. God chose Moses to set the Israelites free from the Egyptians, but Moses lived for years, hidden in plain sight, right in Pharaoh's house. Jesus was and is the Savior of the world, but His public ministry didn't begin until He was 30 years old. Though much focus is given to those latter years of His ministry, those first 29 years mattered greatly, regardless of whether or not anyone else noticed. Never underestimate your value based on where you find yourself today. Your faithfulness now will lead to your greatness later.

Lesson Ten

Use Your
Influence Wisely

*She took of the fruit thereof, and did eat, and gave
also unto her husband with her; and he did eat*
(Genesis 3:6b).

Women are some of the most influential beings that God created on the earth. I am convinced that most women fail to make the most of that quality because they underestimate the power and responsibility of it. The devil is foolish but clever. His plans in the garden were dark, twisted, and well-thought-out. They needed to be, because he was attempting to overthrow God's creation. This creation was not only made in God's image and likeness but also had direct fellowship with God and walked very closely with Him. To succeed, he would need to be subtle and strategic.

One of the most impactful nuggets of wisdom I have received concerning avoiding the traps of the enemy came from a youth pastor at a convention I once attended. He said, "Ask yourself this, if you were Satan, what would you do to try to trip you up. Then master those weaknesses." That strategy holds a lot of wisdom. Satan will indeed customize his attacks to increase the efficiency of his devices. The Bible says to pay attention and be on guard, because the enemy walks around looking for those he can devour (see 1 Pet. 5:8).

Unfortunately, he succeeded with Eve and Adam, and his success came through strategically targeting Eve as a person of influence. We see this dynamic show up in God's conversation with Adam and Eve after they had eaten the fruit:

> *And He said, Who told you that you were naked? Have you eaten of the tree of which I have commanded you that you should not eat? And the man said, The woman whom You gave to be with me—she gave me [fruit] from the tree, and I ate. And the Lord God said to the woman, What is this you have done? And the woman said, the serpent beguiled (cheated, outwitted, and deceived) me, and I ate* (Genesis 3:11–13 AMPC).

The enemy could have gone about tempting Adam and Eve in a variety of ways, but he recognized the power of Eve's influence. He knew that if he could get the woman, then he could get the man. My husband and I have had a running debate for years about who the original sinner in the garden was. Was it Eve (who took the first bite), or was it Adam (who failed to protect her as the man of God)? The Bible only says that Eve was deceived. It does not say Adam was.

We've acknowledged the cushy setup that Eve had before the fall, but Adam's relationship with God predated Eve's. He was God's man. Yet when asked about his sin, he quickly replied, "It was the woman you gave me." Adam completely threw Eve under the bus instead of manning up for his own actions. Yet we must also acknowledge the power of female companionship. Through the generations, Satan has masterfully continued to dumb down the value of a woman in order to wield her influence for his glory. You don't have to allow the enemy to use your influence for his schemes. Stewarding your influence well starts with choosing not to underestimate your influence. Otherwise, you are sure to abuse it.

DON'T BE STRANGE

We find an illustration of this power of influence in Solomon's warning to his son against involvement with "a strange woman":

> *My son, attend unto my wisdom, and bow thine ear to my understanding: That thou mayest regard discretion, and that thy lips may keep knowledge. For the lips of a strange woman drop as an honeycomb, and her mouth is smoother than oil: But her end is bitter as wormwood, sharp as a*

two edged sword. Her feet go down to death; her steps take hold on hell. Lest thou shouldest ponder the path of life, her ways are moveable, that thou canst not know them. Hear me now therefore, O ye children, and depart not from the words of my mouth. Remove thy way far from her, and come not nigh the door of her house: Lest thou give thine honour unto others, and thy years unto the cruel: Lest strangers be filled with thy wealth; and thy labours be in the house of a stranger; And thou morn at the last, when thy flesh and thy body are consumed, And say, How have I hated instruction, and my heart despised reproof; And have not obeyed the voice of my teachers, nor inclined mine ear to them that instructed me (Proverbs 5:1–13).

Often, these verses are presented to point out how a young man can destroy his life by entangling himself with a strange woman. However, when I began my studies for this book, the Lord invited me to take a deeper look. As I did so, I began to see a second life caught in destruction—that of the strange woman. This tragedy was not just for the man who kept company with her but also for the woman who had allowed herself to become so corrupted in the first place.

It got me wondering who this strange woman was and how she got entangled in that lifestyle. She was born into a family, grew up within a community. Yet somehow she allowed herself to be perverted to the point that her ways were leading her to death—and dragging others with her. Or perhaps she was forced into that life and accepted it as her identity. God never intended this life for any woman, but we live in a society today that celebrates it. Satan has done his best to normalize the strangeness of this woman in order to destroy her life *and also* use her as a tool of temptation. A strange woman may receive great praise in the beginning, but the result of her life will be deeply tragic.

Let's read another passage about her from *The Message* paraphrase:

> *As I stood at the window of my house looking out through the shutters, watching the mindless crowd stroll by, I spotted a young man without any sense arriving at the corner of the street where she lived, then turning up the path to her house. It was dusk, the evening coming on, the darkness thickening into night. Just then, a woman met him—she'd been lying in wait for him, dressed to seduce him. Brazen and brash she was, restless and roaming, never at home, walking the streets, loitering in the mall, hanging out at every corner in town. She threw her arms around him and kissed him, boldly took his arm and said, "I've got all the makings for a feast—today I made my offerings, my vows are all paid, so now I've come to find you, hoping to catch sight of your face—and here you are! I've spread fresh, clean sheets on my bed, colorful imported linens. My bed is aromatic with spices and exotic fragrances. Come, let's make love all night, spend the night in ecstatic lovemaking!*

My husband's not home; he's away on business, and he won't be back for a month." Soon she has him eating out of her hand, bewitched by her honeyed speech. Before you know it, he's trotting behind her, like a calf led to the butcher shop, like a stag lured into ambush and then shot with an arrow, like a bird flying into a net not knowing that its flying life is over. So, friends, listen to me, take these words of mine most seriously. Don't fool around with a woman like that; don't even stroll through her neighborhood. Countless victims come under her spell; she's the death of many a poor man. She runs a halfway house to hell, fits you out with a shroud and a coffin (Proverbs 7:6–27 MSG).

Perhaps the most tragic part about this passage is that rather than reading like the stern warning from a loving God that it is meant to be, this reads more like an Oscar-worthy movie or a best-selling novel today. Many a good writer has created so-called art with such indiscretion by just explaining away the backstory of those caught up in this web of sin. Perhaps she's experiencing a midlife crisis. Maybe her marriage is broken. So we celebrate the vigor of the young adulterer caught in the weave of a beautiful yet neglected and lonely vixen who's just finding her wiles again after a loveless existence. We stay fixated to the end, hoping these two find their happy ending together. And let's not forget the climax of the movie, when the husband finds out and there's a fight to the death.

God forbid that this is what we have become, that this is what we allow our children to believe is normal. Music and entertainment have conditioned us to accept this as the sexual empowerment and evolution of a complicated woman—not as the death trap it really is. Our culture tells us to celebrate and admire such a woman. But I say, God forbid!

WORTH MORE

So many women have been introduced to sex improperly—over-exposed, taken advantage of, abused, mistreated and objectified, and so forth. Because of this, many women have severely damaged self-esteems. Satan has used this to cheapen a woman's existence, bring shame into her life, grip her soul with depression, and turn her away from the arms of a loving God. Whatever the backstory of the strange woman in the Bible, ultimately she allowed her experiences to define her and turn her heart away from God:

> *To deliver thee from the strange woman, even from the stranger which flattereth with her words; which forsaketh the guide of her youth, and forgetteth the covenant of her God. For her house inclineth unto death, and her paths unto the dead* (Proverbs 2:16–18).

Even a woman who has allowed herself to become strange was designed to be more than just body parts and curves used to provide sexual pleasure. God did not create her to be someone's garbage can or to trade her influence for acceptance or prosperity. What a waste it is to whittle down such a wonderful gift into mere manipulation tactics. The

spirit behind how you use your influence can often be identified by your motives. Who are you yielding to? Don't forfeit your standards in an attempt to get ahead when you have
already been created at the top of the class.

With great influence comes great responsibility.
Strangeness does not begin when something bad happens
to us but when we close the door to the knowledge and fear
(reverence) of the Lord. Someone else's betrayal does not
have the power to rewrite your story of victory and reduce
your value and splendor. But you do hold that pen, so wield
it wisely. Some of the most financially successful women in
the world today have achieved "greatness" through sex and
seduction. This messaging is all around us. If you want to be
successful, take off your clothes. If you want to attract fol-
lowers, show some skin. Carry yourself seductively. Entice
men, even married ones. Make them desire you and lust for
you so much that they hurl their money at you and compromise their families just to have a taste of you.

Please hear me when I say this—no amount of fame or
money is worth your soul. You were created to be so much
more than that. Sure, people may applaud you in the beginning, and yes, the money may feel nice, but it is damning to
your heart and will cost you the life God has ordained for
you. I feel impressed to say this. I am not highlighting these
truths out of judgment, but I feel compelled by the great
love of the Father to expose the lies that the enemy has been
using to steal the crowns of God's beautiful queens.

I can almost hear some women being offended at me
right now, saying I am excusing the behaviors of shady men

and blaming it all on women. That is not true, but I am speaking to the heart of every woman and exhorting her to not allow Satan to steal anything else from her life. We are each responsible for the actions we take (both men and women), and God will hold each of us accountable for our choices—whether we heeded the wisdom of God or succumbed to the rebellion of the enemy. However, let that not distract us from the lesson we can learn from Mother Eve. Don't allow Satan to evict you out of your garden and use your beautiful influence to fulfill his hateful agenda. I don't care how popular or normalized sin may be. When you forfeit God's standards, you are most certainly forfeiting your crown.

I am convinced that great pain and disappointment lead many women down this dark path. So many strange women are queens who have traded their influence in hopes of filling the voids left by past betrayals. No amount of sin, or the praise that comes from it, can ever fill those holes. It will only deepen them. That's the deception. It's a trap, a black hole designed to swallow your hope, your value, and your life.

But God! He is the mender of the brokenhearted. He is full of compassion and mercy. He sent His Son, Jesus, to not only restore you back to the beauty that Eve forfeited but to also erase the shame and stench of your past life. You may have never been able to trust any man, but you can trust God. He sees you for who you really are: His queen. Stop looking in the mirror with disgust and start seeing the wonderful woman He has chosen, the woman He loves despite your mistakes. Jesus died to get rid of yesterday and to make your future bright. This is His mission statement:

The Spirit of the Lord is upon Me, because He has anointed Me to preach the gospel to the poor; He has sent me to heal the brokenhearted, to proclaim liberty to the captives and recovery of sight to the blind, to set at liberty those who are oppressed; to proclaim the acceptable year of the Lord (Luke 4:18–19 NKJV).

Reverse the plan that the enemy has tried to deploy in your life, and accept the freedom that comes in Christ, knowing that God has you. Use your influence and your testimony to bring people to Him so that they may also be set free. You don't have to give away your soul to attain something that's already been purchased for you. You are powerful, and you are here for a reason. God has great plans for you, and He will use you mightily if you let Him. But make no mistake about this fact: You will never be more loved than you are right now. You aren't walking with Him to gain His love; He's already freely given His love to you. The Bible says that even while we were dead in our sins, Christ saw fit to die for us (see Rom. 5:8). We don't have to perform to obtain His love. Instead, we get to walk with Him and learn to live as women who are already *so* loved—not rejected. "For God so loved the world that He gave His only begotten Son, that whosoever believeth in him should not perish, but have everlasting life" (John 3:16).

MIND YOUR WORDS

Behold, we put bits in the horses' mouths, that they may obey us; and we turn about their whole body. Behold also the ships, which though they be

so great, and are driven of fierce winds, yet are
they turned about with a very small helm, whith-
ersoever the governor listeth. Even so the tongue
is a little member, and boasteth great things.
Behold, how great a matter a little fire kindleth!
And the tongue is a fire, a world of iniquity: so is
the tongue among our members, that it defileth
the whole body, and setteth on fire the course of
nature; and it is set on fire of hell (James 3:3–6).

One of your greatest tools of influence is found right in your mouth. The tongue is an incredible weapon that has the power to produce great blessing or great destruction. It is small but it is powerful. As a result, it is easy to underestimate the potential consequences of an untamed tongue. "Words kill, words give life; they're either poison or fruit— you choose" (Prov. 18:21 MSG). Make no mistake about it, what you say matters. Each day, the words you choose to utter to others and to yourself can affect the quality of your life and theirs. As Peter wrote, "For he that will love life, and see good days, let him refrain his tongue from evil, and his lips that they speak no guile" (1 Pet. 3:10).

We live in a society today that promotes gossip and celebrates careless and critical speech. Tabloids, talk shows, entertainment shows, and comedians, to name a few, often increase their popularity by attacking, slandering, and making fun of other people. The paparazzi swirl around the famous, looking to catch some private bit of information that they can use as entertainment for the masses. These practices have been normalized in our culture. It's normal to be critical, to gossip, to curse, and to tear down others. This mass desensitization has caused many to misuse the influence the Lord has given them and to negatively impact their world. Regardless of whether everyone else is doing it, we will each individually give an account on how we have chosen to use our mouths. Jesus warned:

> *But I say unto you, that every idle word that men shall speak, they shall give account thereof in the day of judgement. For by thy words thou shalt be justified, and by thy words thou shalt be condemned* (Matthew 12:36–37).

This is one of the reasons that the Word tells us to continually renew our minds to the Word of God (see Rom. 12:1–2). If our thoughts line up with God's Word, then our words are sure to follow. We are all like sponges; whatever is soaked up is what will come out when the pressures of life arise.

> *A good man out of the good treasure of his heart brings forth good; and an evil man out of the evil treasure of his heart brings forth evil. For out of the abundance of the heart his mouth speaks* (Luke 6:45 NKJV).

We have spent a great deal of time discussing the importance of guarding our hearts, but it still bears repeating: What you allow to settle into your soul and your mind can be the difference between a life of joy and peace and a life of destruction and deprivation. Always strive to keep the conditions of your heart pure and guard your thought life. What you think on leads to what you will say and do. What you say and do will lead to what you experience in this life.

THE POWER TO DESTROY

Words have the power to hurt and harm. James uses the word *fire* to describe the tongue. Fires often start off small and can quickly grow to become an enormous inferno. Even the smallest of words can have a lifetime effect on the hearer. I am sure we have all spoken words that we wish we could take back, but the truth is, they cannot be taken back. Many beautiful relationships have been destroyed by a few unwise words that led to major wars. "The words of the reckless pierce like swords, but the tongue of the wise brings healing" (Prov. 12:18 NIV).

During the first few years of my marriage, I noticed that a certain compliment seemed to make my husband feel uncomfortable. I am head over heels in love with him. He is a beautiful man both inside and out with lovely dark chocolate skin, which is one of my favorite things about him. His skin tone is amazing, and I often tell him that. However, in the beginning, his responses to those compliments were sheepish and downright awkward. After witnessing his response over several occasions, I sat down with him to inquire about it. To my surprise, he began to share about his childhood school years. He shared how he was often the darkest skinned person in his class and that the children relentlessly teased him and made fun of his complexion. It turned out that my preference for his skin color directly challenged an inward insecurity that had formed as a result of those children's insults all those years ago. Words, indeed, are powerful.

This is why Paul counsels:

> *Do not let any unwholesome talk come out of your mouths, but only what is helpful for building others up according to their needs, that it may benefit those who listen* (Ephesians 4:29 NIV).

When we allow ungodly communication to fill our tongue, we are doing the opposite of bringing benefit to the listener. We are, in fact, bringing destruction. Beware of the words you speak to your children, your friends, your spouse, and your loved ones; your words are either adding to or subtracting from their wellness.

Another characteristic about fire that is worth noting is that fire will only burn if fuel is feeding it. "Without wood a fire goes out; without gossip a quarrel dies down" (Prov. 26:20 NIV). When fire has fuel, it will quickly reproduce itself. That's how gossip grows: *quickly.* Have you ever played the game where you start with a phrase that is whispered one by one down through a line of people? By the time it gets to the last person, often the phrase has been completely altered. When you engage in gossip, what may have started off as something small can take on a life of its own, leaving pain and destruction in its wake. Not only are you engaging foolishly, but you are fueling strife and mischief that often is difficult to reverse. "The words of a gossip are like choice morsels; they go down to the inmost parts" (Prov. 18:8 NIV).

Fires thrive on oxygen, and they quickly dissipate when that source is removed. Any significant relationship will have disagreements. We still live in a fallen world, and inevitably squabbles arise. You may not have started the fire, but what you put into it determines the ferocity of it. "A soft answer turns away wrath, but a harsh word stirs up anger" (Prov. 15:1 NKJV). It is so easy, in a heated moment, to feel justified in shooting your mouth off and inflicting the pain you are feeling on the other person. However, even in a heated argument, you have great influence, and you have a choice about how you use it. Sure, you can keep the insults coming, but the damage of words sown in anger can be the death of the relationships God has given you. Your response is crucial to extinguishing the flames that are intent on destroying your life. "Sin is not ended by multiplying words, but the prudent hold their tongues" (Prov. 10:19 NIV).

THE GRACE TO BUILD

A word fitly spoken is like apples of gold in pictures of silver (Proverbs 25:11).

A beautiful way to use your influence is to use your words to build others up. It not only brings healing to their souls but to yours as well. I love the description of this verse, as I can envision apples of gold surrounded by silver. To get the full scope of this verse, I looked up some benefits associated with apples. They are nutritious, support weight loss, provide benefit to the heart, reduce risk of disease, promote gut health, and help to protect the brain. Wow! What amazing context that brings to wise words. They provide substance and help the hearer to drop old weights that have plagued them just like my compliments were doing for my husband. Your wise words can promote healing in their hearts and in their gut by flushing out the negativity of the past. Last, you can positively affect their thoughts and help prevent mental and emotional illness in their lives. That alone is worth filling our mouths with the sweetness and the love of God.

Gold and silver are both desirable and expensive. They are highly sought-after commodities that many are eager to possess. Likewise, kind and encouraging words are valuable and desirable. They are royal and majestic, just like every person is in God's eyes. I used to be a very critical person. One of the ways I overcame that was to remind myself, when dealing with challenging people, that God loves them just as much as He loves me. They are no less valuable to Him then I am; they are merely hurting people with a different perspective than my own. As a wise man once said, *hurting people hurt people.*

Many hurting people are around us; a few kind words can go a long way in their lives. Many are living with discouragement and depression, but an encouraging word can provide a spark of life to their wearied souls. We saw earlier that the tongue of the wise can bring healing to the hearer (see Prov. 12:18b). Oh how beautiful it is to have the ability to spread love and healing to those around us. Please don't take that for granted. You have a gift on the inside of you to help uplift and encourage those around you, especially your children. As parents, we have been entrusted by God to wisely build up our offspring. God has graced and gifted each child, and though they may be challenging at times, we are called to speak life into them, not death. Many hurting adults struggle in their daily lives because of the dissenting words spoken over them as children. In that same manner, we can raise strong children who will flourish as adults because of the godly and encouraging words spoken over them. "The soothing tongue is a tree of life, but a perverse tongue crushes the spirit" (Prov. 15:4 NIV).

Perhaps *you* are the one who could use life spoken into you. Never underestimate the power of your tongue over your life. Maybe you're not in an uplifting environment, but you can look in the mirror and encourage yourself. The words you hear have a great effect on your heart, so put God's Word in your mouth and speak it often and loudly so that you may hear it and be comforted. Use your influence wisely, even over yourself, and allow God to build the great queen that He has birthed in you.

Sin Costs Too Much

And Adam knew Eve his wife; and she conceived, and bare Cain, and said, I have gotten a man from the Lord. And she again bare his brother Abel. And Abel was a keeper of sheep, but Cain was a tiller of the ground. And in process of time it came to pass, that Cain brought of the fruit of the ground an offering unto the Lord. And Abel, he also brought of the firstlings of his flock and of the fat thereof. And the Lord had respect unto Abel and to his offering: But unto Cain and to his offering he had not respect. And Cain was very wroth, and his countenance fell. And the Lord said unto Cain, Why are thou wroth? and why is thy countenance fallen? If thou doest well, shalt thou not be accepted? and if thou doest not well, sin lieth at the door. And unto thee shall be his desire, and thou shalt rule over him. And Cain talked with Abel his brother, and it came to pass, when they were in the field, that Cain rose up against Abel his brother, and slew him (Genesis 4:1–8).

What a tragedy this was for Eve. I cannot begin to imagine how painful it must have been for Eve to lose her son Abel. This pain was undoubtedly intensified by the fact that Abel's life was taken by her other son, Cain. No mother should have to face such a reality. That grief and loss were never intended for her, but Satan was happy to immerse her in it. She had given him influence in her life, and death was the painful result. Sin will always cost you more than you intend to pay.

SATAN DOES NOT PLAY FAIR

When Eve was conversing with the serpent, she could not have imagined all the destruction Satan had lined up for her. She had no idea that the consequences of that decision would span out so far, even affecting the sons she had not yet borne. That fruit looked good and seemed like a worthy risk, but here, years later, the effects of sin entering the world had once again produced such tremendous grief. Satan is cruel and heartless. If you give him an inch, he will take a mile.

When I was a child, I went through some rebellious years. My parents were strict but fair. They did a great job communicating with my siblings and me not just what they expected of us but also what consequences awaited us if we chose to disobey. I remember, especially in my teen years, sitting on my bed contemplating breaking the rules. I used to try to calculate what the punishment would be to decide if it was worth it. I even remember one time thinking to myself, *This is going to land me in big trouble, so I better make it good.* At the time, I thought I was being smart, like I was going to figure out how to have my fun. Now it is so easy to see the foolishness behind such calculations.

But too often we approach God's instructions this way, saying, "Oh, it's not that deep." "This will be worth it." "God knows I have needs, so He understands." Meanwhile, we fail to understand that the enemy's plans for us are much more than a moment of sin. He wants to snuff out your life and your future; don't let him!

GOD IS A LOVER, NOT A HATER

My parents raised me in the Word of God since birth. I even attended Rhema Bible Training Center with my parents for the first three months of my life, because I was born on spring break when they were students. I started out with a strong foundation. However, in my younger years, I often caught myself feeling that God was in some ways a bit of a *hater*—someone who liked to come in and spoil all the fun. In my years in ministry, I've encountered many people who approach the standards of God in the same light—like a boring old set of rules.

But let me share this nugget that changed my whole perspective: God is a lover, not a hater. Eve may have felt like eating that fruit wasn't a big deal. It was just one bite. Maybe she even thought, *Why did He create the tree in the first place?* But God's motives toward us have been clear since day one: "And God blessed them, and God said unto them, Be fruitful, and multiply, and replenish the earth, and subdue it" (Gen. 1:28a). His plan is and has always been to bless us. He wants us to experience His multiplication, not the subtraction that comes at the hand of the enemy.

God is like a mother who has babyproofed her home so that her children cannot electrocute themselves. Is she hating on their fun? No, she is protecting her children. Sin produces death. God's love for you has always been to pardon you from that death. That's why He has so freely supplied His Word to us to allow us to experience the joy, growth, and freedom that reside in His will for us. He loves us so deeply—so much so that even after the great mess-up that allowed sin to infiltrate our nature, God sent His Son, Jesus, to redeem us so that we can still have access, through His grace and mercy, to abundant life.

Do not repeat Eve's mistakes. Do not let yourself see the boundaries of God as anything other than love and protection. That is what they are. God's love and kindness toward us are constant:

> *For the mountains shall depart, and the hills be removed; but my kindness shall not depart from thee, neither shall the covenant of my peace be removed, saith the Lord that hath mercy on thee* (Isaiah 54:10).

WHO TOLD YOU THAT YOU WERE NAKED?

Sin is dangerous, not only because it steals, but also because it makes cowards of men.

> *And the Lord God called unto Adam, and said unto him, Where art thou? And he said, I heard thy voice in the garden, and I was afraid, because I was naked; and I hid myself. And he said, Who told thee that thou wast naked? Hast thou eaten of the tree, whereof I commanded thee that thou shouldest not eat?* (Genesis 3:9–11).

This passage in Genesis shows us something interesting about Adam. His response to God, when God was searching for him, was a clue that led God right to the problem. How did God know to ask about the tree? Adam admitted that fear and shame had caused him to hide *because he was naked.* But earlier, before the fall, Adam and Eve were both naked, and they were not ashamed (see Gen. 2:25). The nakedness wasn't new. But something else had changed—the glory.

Once they stepped into sin, their senses were suddenly opened to the lies and whims of the enemy. God asked Adam, "Who told you that you were naked?" In other words, "Who have you been talking to?" These questions are still worthy of being asked today. Who told you that you are sick? Who told you that you are disgusting? Who told you that you will never be worth anything? Who told you that you will never get married? Who told you that you are unlovable? And why are you listening to them?

So many people accept the lies of the enemy because they don't believe they are worthy of the glory of God. They allow their past failures and sins to justify the captivity they live in, never receiving the freedom provided for them in Christ. We no longer have to be bonded to the mistakes of our past. We don't have to feel that shame and nakedness anymore. Not because we are so great, but because Jesus came to restore the glory of God upon our lives. He came to revive the confidence we were created with. You don't have to accept the death associated with sin; you can place it under the blood of Jesus and live life anew.

The apostle Paul made this clear in 2 Corinthians 5:17–21:

> *Therefore if anyone is in Christ [that is, grafted in, joined to Him by faith in Him as Savior], he is a new creature [reborn and renewed by the Holy Spirit]; the old things [the previous moral and spiritual condition] have passed away. Behold, new things have come [because spiritual awakening brings a new life]. But all these things are from God, who reconciled us to Himself through Christ [making us acceptable to Him] and gave us the ministry of reconciliation [so that by our example we might bring others to Him], that is, that God was in Christ reconciling the world to Himself, not counting people's sins against them [but cancelling them]. And He has committed to us the message of reconciliation [that is, restoration to favor with God]. So we are ambassadors for*

Christ, as though God were making His appeal through us; we [as Christ's representatives] plead with you on behalf of Christ to be reconciled to God. He made Christ who knew no sin to [judicially] be sin on our behalf, so that in Him we would become the righteousness of God [that is, we would be made acceptable to Him and placed in a right relationship with Him by His gracious loving kindness] (AMP).

A WORD OF CAUTION

Through His great sacrifice, Jesus has given us such a wonderful gift. If we repent of our sins, He is faithful to forgive us (see 1 John 1:9). The ultimate price was paid for us. Now, the best thing you can do as a believer is to learn to be a good judge—of yourself. Some still find themselves wrapped up in the destruction of sin because they fail to judge themselves wisely. The Bible says, "For if we would judge ourselves, we should not be judged. But when we are judged, we are chastened of the Lord, that we should not be condemned with the world" (1 Cor. 11:31–32).

Sin unchecked will make a fool out of you, and we have already discussed the fate of a fool. It may start off small, but if left unchecked, even the smallest shortcomings can cost you big dividends. Many of us can relate to this in our attempts to preserve our own bodies. Many people have annual physicals with their doctor whether they are feeling ill or not. The point is to snuff out any issues while they are small and manageable so that they do not grow into life-threatening diseases. We should carry that same diligence into judging ourselves. Think of it as giving yourself a regular checkup. The story of Samson in the Old Testament is a great example of this principle. He was in dire need of a self-checkup, but his neglect cost him his life.

Samson's start was a supernatural one (see Judg. 13). His mother had been barren when the angel of the Lord appeared to her with a promise and instructions.

> *For behold, you shall conceive and bear a son. And no razor shall come upon his head, for the child shall be a Nazirite to God from the womb; and he shall begin to deliver Israel out of the hand of the Philistines* (Judges 13:5 NKJV).

Once again, like we have seen in the story of Eve, the promise of God came with some boundaries. One of those was that Samson's hair was not to be cut. If someone had approached Samson with a razor, he would have quickly identified and eliminated that threat. But, as we see in the subtleness of the serpent with Eve, Satan rarely presents himself in an obvious manner. He will disguise himself as whatever he believes will be most effective in tricking you into destroying yourself. In Samson's case, his serpent was a woman named Delilah. These next several verses show how badly Samson needed a self-checkup.

> *Afterward it happened that he loved a woman in the Valley of Sorek, whose name was Delilah. And the lords of the Philistines came up to her and said to her, "Entice him, and find out where his great strength lies, and by what means we may*

overpower him, that we may bind him to afflict him; and everyone of us will give you eleven hundred pieces of silver" (Judges 16:4–5 NKJV).

I imagine this part of the story as the stethoscope part of a checkup, because it listens to the heartbeat. Clearly, Samson's heart was beating for a woman from his enemy's camp. *Is your heart beating for the right things?* This wasn't the first time Samson got caught with an ungodly woman (see Judg. 14:1–3). Clearly this was an ongoing and unchecked issue in Samson's life, and now he was entangled with a serious devil in a dress. Not everything that is pleasing to you is good for you. Sin is enticing because it seems good for a time, but Samson's "good time" cost him everything.

> *So Delilah said to Samson, "Please tell me where your great strength lies, and with what you may be bound to afflict you." And Samson said unto her, "If they bind me with seven fresh bowstrings, not yet dried, then I shall become weak and be like any other man." So the lords of the Philistines brought up to her seven fresh bowstrings, not yet dried, and she bound him with them* (Judges 16:7–8 NKJV).

I like to call this the thermometer portion of the self-checkup. *Do you have a fever?* Clearly, Samson did. Some people are enticed by the danger element. It did not take a rocket scientist to figure out this woman was trouble. However, I believe Samson found some sport in playing with fire. I always scratch my head when I hear people boast about the parties they will throw when they get to hell, like they're looking forward to it. They are deceived and do not know it. The Bible says that when a man is tempted, he is drawn away by his own desires and lust and enticed to sin, which leads to death (see James 1:13–15). Check your temperature and find out what has you hot. If you're on fire for God, great; but if you are driven by ungodly desires, do yourself a favor and get that temperature down.

> *Now men were lying in wait, staying with her in the room and she said to him, "The Philistines are upon you, Samson!" But he broke the bowstrings as a standoff yarn breaks when it touches fire. So the secret of his strength was not known* (Judges 16:9 NKJV).

Samson made the mistake so many still make today—continuing to sin because he didn't feel the consequences. It's clear that his relationship with this woman was an ungodly one. I would assume he had been counseled against it. Yet he continued to play with fire because he had yet to be burned. When he woke up to find the Philistines on the attack, he still had his strength. Many people continue in sin because they feel that, like Samson, *they still got it.* However, do not mistake the mercy of God on your life for thinking that He is alright with your sin. Sometimes God's grace is giving you time to change your mind about what you are doing. Make no mistake about it, payday comes for us all.

> *Then Delilah said to Samson, "Look, you have mocked me and told me lies. Now please tell me what you may be bound with"* (Judges 16:10 NKJV).

This is the weigh-in part of the checkup. As we see in Samson's life, when you live your life according to your flesh, it will add undesirable weights in hopes of dragging you down. Your flesh will always accept death. How did Samson fail to recognize that this woman was trying to kill him? Not only had she tried to have him killed, but she was also upset with him that it didn't work. An anointed man of God was weighed down with stupidity, blinded by his own lust. In verses 11–14, Delilah tried two more times to kill him to no avail. This leads us to his fateful decision:

> *Then she said to him, "How can you say, 'I love you,' when your heart is not with me? You have mocked me these three times and have not told me where your great strength lies"* (Judges 16:15 NKJV).

I equate this verse to the blood draw portion of a good physical. As the doctors draw blood to check the levels of their patient, Delilah too was drawing on Samson by challenging his commitment level to her. Her manipulation was so evident; she questioned his love for her while also betraying him by the murder attempts. *What are your levels saying?*

> *It came to pass, when she pestered him daily with her words and pressed him, so that his soul was vexed to death, that he told her all of his heart, and said to her, "No razor has ever come upon my head, for I have been a Nazirite to God from my mother's womb. If I am shaven, then my strength will leave me, and I shall become weak, and be like any other man"* (Judges 16:16–17 NKJV).

This is the blood pressure point of the checkup. This woman put so much pressure on him that he gave in. As we discussed in a previous chapter, peer pressure is dangerous. Samson shouldn't have been with this woman on a daily basis, but he allowed that ungodly pressure to build up, and as a result, that strange woman shaved his head, and his strength left him (see Judg. 16:18–19). Samson failed his physical and ended up in the hands of his enemies. *Are your pressures under control?*

> *Then the Philistines took him and put out his eyes and brought him down to Gaza. They bound him with bronze fetters, and he became a grinder in the prison* (Judges 16:21 NKJV).

Samson's life is a cautionary tale about the importance of judging yourself by the Word of God. Satan is still using the same tactics today. He will dress up death in the most attractive package in attempts to stop you, but he cannot succeed when you are vigilant about yourself. He still seeks to deceive, kill, and destroy, but God is for you. He has given you His Word and dominion over even the enemy.

God's great grace and mercy have afforded you the ability to walk in the victory Jesus Christ provided, but do not use that as an excuse to sin. God knows the intents and purposes of the heart; a truly delivered individual will desire to please God, not take advantage of Him. Paul talked about this issue several times in his letter to the Galatians.

> *For you, my brothers, were called to freedom; only do not let your freedom become an opportunity for the sinful nature (worldliness, selfishness),*

but through love serve and seek the best for one another (Galatians 5:13 AMP).

And he added, "Be not deceived; God is not mocked: for whatsoever a man soweth, that shall he also reap" (Gal. 6:7). We all make mistakes. We do still live in a fallen world. But God knows the difference between genuine mistakes and a rebellious spirit.

If your heart desire is to honor God, then take heart! He will not hold your mistakes against you. The God of the universe has restored you to right relationship with Him. Through His Son, the road to your victory has been paved. Walk it out in godly confidence and be the light He has created you to be in a dark world.

WHAT TO DO WHEN YOU MESS UP

The apostle Paul said, "For all have sinned, and come short of the glory of God" (Rom. 3:22). Each one of us messes up from time to time. Even when our hearts are yielded to God, mistakes happen. We are imperfect beings living in a fallen world, so learning how to have a proper recovery is paramount. Many people don't know how to respond when they mess up, and they get tossed further into sin because of their guilt and shame. But that doesn't have to be your story. Here are ten tips to help you successfully recover after a mess-up.

First, *accept responsibility for your mistake and don't sweep it under the rug.* "If we confess our sins, he is faithful and just to forgive us our sins, and to cleanse us from all unrighteousness" (1 John 1:9).

Second, *get back up again.* "For a just man falleth seven times, and riseth up again: but the wicked shall fall into mischief" (Prov. 24:16). It's important to not let guilt get you stuck in a rut. The blood of Jesus has made it possible for you to bounce right back, so get to it.

Third, *don't run from God; run to Him.* It's only natural to run away when you have betrayed someone. Adam and Eve hid in the garden because of their sins, but through the blood of Jesus we can still come boldly to the throne of grace and receive mercy and help when we need it (see Heb. 4:16).

Fourth, *don't misplace your anger and blame others for your mistake.* Simply put, don't be Cain about it (see Gen. 4:1–8). Don't create new mistakes by operating in jealousy, envy, or offense with people.

Fifth, *learn to ask for help.* Sometimes we need to lay down our pride and ask for assistance. You were never meant to live on an island. Asking for help does not mean that you are weak but instead that you are strong. Many people allow their pride to keep them drowning, even when they are surrounded by the life rafts of other people. Don't be one of those people.

Sixth, *let God write your detour plan.* Sometimes God's recovery plan is getting you back to the basics, which is not always exciting. Don't be an adrenaline junkie who lives on the edge and looks for new things when you have not mastered the foundations. "Finally, my brethren, rejoice in the Lord. To write the same things to you, to me indeed is not grievous, but for you it is safe" (Phil. 3:1).

Seventh, *don't let your repentance be for a honeymoon period.* There is a difference between true repentance and just being sad you got caught. Be sure to keep your heart and your motives in check.

Eighth, *believe for the comfort of the Holy Ghost while the dust settles.* The consequences of sin can be uncomfortable and can create unwanted circumstances along with guilt. Don't seek comfort in the enemy's camp, which will only get you caught in a cycle of sin. The blood of Jesus covered your sin, so while you're walking through the aftermath, lean on the Holy Spirit to get you through. God is a wonderful friend "who comforts us in all our tribulation, that we may be able to comfort those who are in any trouble, with the comfort with which we ourselves are comforted by God" (2 Cor. 1:4 NKJV).

Ninth, *release your faith in God's ability to fix it.* If God could fix Adam and Eve's mess, which affected the whole world, then surely He can handle yours. He is a restorer, even when you don't deserve it.

Tenth, *learn to believe in yourself again.* Sometimes our greatest enemy is our inner self and the disgust we feel about our actions. This can be hard to overcome. But don't allow your shortcomings to override the righteousness of God in you. Make a quality decision to agree with God about yourself. It doesn't matter how you feel or what others say; make God the final say. He loved you unchanged and loves you too much to leave you unchanged. He has grace enough to help you overcome and walk in the life of Christ again.

But God, who is rich in mercy, because of His great love with which He loved us, even when we were dead in trespasses, made us alive together with Christ (by grace you have been saved), and raised up together, and made us sit together in the heavenly places in Christ Jesus (Ephesians 2:4–6 NKJV).

Lesson Twelve

Beauty for Ashes

Because thou hast done this, thou art cursed above all cattle, and above every beast of the field; upon thy belly shalt thou go, and dust shalt thou eat all the days of thy life: And I will put enmity between thee and the woman, and between thy seed and her seed; it shall bruise thy head, and thou shalt bruise his heel (Genesis 3:14–15).

As you enter this last chapter, I want to encourage you to really open your heart. We have spent a lot of time discussing the beautiful Eve and her fall. We have all felt the consequences of her decision. However, I am thankful for what her story has imparted to my own life. As I end this book, I want to focus on what I consider the most beautiful part of this story—God's response to her mess-up. In human relationships, if you want to have a good relationship with someone, you'd better treat that person the right way. If you want people to go out of their way for you, have a space for you, and consider you, then you need to make sure to do all the things needed to deserve that. We understand the human type of love that says "I'm here if I am happy with you." However, God's love for Eve (and for all of us) is so far above the conditional human emotion we call love.

THE PLAN

It blows my mind how quickly God set up His plan—not to get back at Eve for her mess, but to bring restoration to what would have otherwise been a hopeless aftermath. God, in His holiness, could have scrapped humankind altogether and moved on to a new venture. But that's not who He is. He is tenderhearted, loving, and compassionate. This final lesson might be my all-time favorite lesson from Eve as it is the lesson that I draw upon day after day after day. This is the truth that delivered me from the darkness of my past and my own insecurities, and it even inspired me to write this book.

When you mess up and are undeserving, when you have flat out blown it for no good reason, when you've gone left when you should have gone right, when you've run away when you should have trusted, when you've turned your back when you should have stayed in faith—God is willing to take all that mess and give you *beauty* for those *ashes*.

In God's curse upon the serpent for his part in the great mess-up, we find something beautiful. At first glance, it may look like the serpent is just getting what was coming to him. He deserved a life sentence. But in God's discussion of the relationship between the serpent and the woman (and her seed), we find God's mercy for humanity. God had not even handed out the consequences of their actions to Adam and Eve, yet here He shows His hand of mercy toward them while cursing the serpent. The seed of woman will bruise the serpent's head even though the serpent would bruise his heel. This verse is crucial because it's the first time we see God's redemptive intent. God would have been well within His rights to do away with humanity, but His love for us created a different plan. His plan meant He saw *past* the big mess-up to an even bigger redemption.

Imagine the shame and anguish Eve must have felt as she stood before God, realizing what she had done. Yet in that moment, God spoke a word into existence that would bring redemption and restoration. He used this moment of shame for the man and woman to release a word that would fix it all. How beautiful and how gracious! God put His anger aside and declared a way forward, a path of restoration back to what Adam and Eve had forfeited. God did not leave Eve in her mess, and He will not leave you in yours.

Not only did God speak that plan, but He revealed that He would use a woman again in His plan. One might think that after Eve started this mess, God would steer clear of women. Instead, He used a daughter of Eve, the virgin Mary, to bring Jesus into this world. And Jesus went to the cross, bore our sickness and diseases, and paid the price—not just for Adam and Eve's sins, but for all of our sins. Satan indeed bruised His heel with that crucifixion plan, and Jesus gave up His life and went to hell for three days. For three days it looked bad. For three days I'm sure it felt hopeless. For three days the enemy rejoiced. But at the end of those three days, Jesus arose with great power and *crushed the head of the enemy!*

Some of us are stuck in the shame of our sins because we think God is mad at us. It's so easy and almost natural to run away from God when we mess up. It is so hard to look people in the eye when you know you've done them wrong. But God is not mad at you; He is eager to turn those burnt-up ashes into beauty.

Later in Genesis 3, as we see Adam and Eve's consequences come to fruition, we can still see the compassionate nature of God. Even as He drove them from the garden, we learn that He did not do it in anger but in love. He needed to ensure they would not eat of the tree of life and make their death a permanent condition. Adam and Eve had sewn together fig leaves to cover themselves, since they had lost their glory, but God made better clothes for them, even as they were walking out the consequences of their actions. He didn't have to do that. He wanted to because He loved them. He is a loving God, and He loves you. You don't need to wait until you're all cleaned up to run to Him. Come running just as you are—with all of the hurt, pain, failure, sadness, and ashes—and watch Him transform them into beauty.

DON'T GIVE UP NOW

Maybe you are reading this book thinking, *That all sounds nice, but it's just too late for me.* Maybe you feel like you just can't take another step, that life has beaten you down so much that you no longer even know who you are. Let me say this to you: You have come too far to give up now! It is no coincidence that you are reading this book. God has aligned this moment and had these words printed on these pages just for you. The God of the universe, who is tasked with so many things, is here right now calling you out of the muck and mire and out of the pit of despair, because you don't belong there. Maybe your own bad decisions put you there, but no matter. The blood of Jesus redeems it all. The issue is not whether you deserve His love and forgiveness; the issue is whether you will receive it.

AGAIN

Sometimes it is very difficult to move past the pain and problems of the past when we are the cause of the problems we are facing. In the previous chapter, we discussed the great Samson and how Delilah took him down, but there's another part of his story that I would like to show you.

> *But the Philistines took him, and put out his eyes, and brought him down to Gaza, and bound him with fetters of brass; and he did grind in the prison house. Howbeit the hair of his head began to grow again after he was shaven* (Judges 16:21–22).

There's no argument that Samson's issues were a result of his own lust, something he could have dealt with long before Delilah came along and shaved his hair. I can only imagine what Samson was feeling in that prison as he lay there tricked and defeated, chained and destitute. I am sure many of us have had moments like these in our own lives on the other end of bad decisions. However, I want to point out a very important word in verse 22. This word brings hope to hopeless situations and strength to weary hearts. That word is *again*.

After all that had been done, all the mistakes that had been made, all the consequences of those bad mistakes, the hair on Samson's head began to grow *again*. He asked the Lord to renew his strength one more time, and God strengthened him *again*. As a result, Samson slew more of his enemies in his death than he had in his entire life (see Judges 16:28–30). We indeed serve a God of *again*. He is kind, and He is merciful. "It is of the Lord's mercies that we are not consumed, because his compassions fail not. They are new every morning: great is thy faithfulness" (Lam. 3:22–23).

If you find yourself in a mess, regardless of how you got there, know that God is faithful to forgive, restore, and bless you *again*. We tend to struggle with that word *again*, because we know we don't deserve it. We've all faced circumstances that, when we look back, we can say, "I should have been stronger. I should have handled it better. I should have been better." However, that word *again* speaks of commitment. It denotes God's faithfulness toward us in good times and bad times. You may be facing many struggles in your life. Maybe you feel dried-up. But let me encourage you by saying, *there is hope for you yet.*

Consider a story in the Old Testament in which God brought life back into a dead situation.

The hand of the Lord was on me, and he brought me out by the Spirit of the Lord and set me in the middle of the valley; it was full of bones. He led me back and forth among them, and I saw a great many bones on the floor of the valley, bones that were very dry. He asked me, "Son of man, can these bones live?" I said, "Sovereign Lord, you alone know." Then he said to me, "Prophesy to these bones and say to them, 'Dry bones, hear the word of the Lord! This is what the Sovereign Lord says to these bones: I will make breath enter you, and you will come to life. I will attach tendons to you and make flesh come upon you and cover you with skin; I will put breath in you, and you will come to life. Then you will know that I am the Lord'" (Ezekiel 37:1–6 NIV).

These dry bones represented a whole group of people: the children of Israel. As a nation, they had fallen on very trying times, which left them hopeless and destitute. The situation was so dire that the bones weren't just dead, but they had been dead for so long that decomposition had set in, leaving dry and brittle bones behind. I don't know if you've ever walked through a season that felt like this, but take comfort in God's response. There is significance in the phrase "the hand of the Lord." The hand is used to touch. Often, when things are this bad, people tend to shy away, but God chooses to get involved. He will do this in your life with His personal touch.

He also brought Ezekiel out of the natural realm into the spirit realm. I'd like to draw your attention to two things here. First, to be brought or carried by someone denotes a strong movement that occurs using the strength of another and without the action of the carried. Praise God, you may feel that your strength is gone, but He will carry you through. Second, it is significant that God revealed Himself not in the natural realm but the spiritual. Sometimes you must change the lens you're looking with and get your eyes off what you're seeing naturally. Things look very different in the spirit.

The valley in this passage signifies a place of vulnerability. When you feel surrounded on every side by mounds of trouble, you are most likely walking through a valley like this. Often, enemies seem to gain the advantage in the valley. It's often very cold because the sun is blocked by the surrounding mountains. If the effects of the valley aren't enough, it's also full of dry and brittle bones. Those bones represent things that affect the core of one's being like sad memories, lost opportunities, grief, darkness, disappointment, devastation, and so forth. But what's remarkable is that God initiated the restoration. Sometimes we feel as if no one sees what we are going through, but God does. He not only sees what's on the surface, but He gets down into the depths to bring restoration.

Bones, by nature, are foundational to the body. The enemy would like nothing more than to destroy your foundation. However, neither the enemy nor other people can determine your potential. In verse 3, God asked Ezekiel, "Can these bones live?" God is a miracle-working God, and He wants to restore the dry bones in your life. He is a rebuilder and simply cannot resist a good resurrection. Your life may look like that valley of dry bones, but God sees potential. God's instructions to Ezekiel included speaking to the dry bones. The same goes for you. Speak to that hopelessness, speak to that lack, speak to your own broken heart, and proclaim what God will do. Have faith in God's Word rather than in what you see. Stop listening to your feelings and hear the Word of the Lord. *He will restore.* Say that whenever you are tempted to give up.

God said several things to the dry bones. First, He called breath back into them and changed their status from death back to life. God wants you to live *again.* He wants you to dream *again,* and He wants you to love *again.* Receive that for your life. Second, He said He would attach tendons back to the bone. A tendon is connective tissue that usually connects muscle to bone. As a result, it can withstand tension. Tendons function to transmit forces and store energy that allows them to restore and recover at high efficiency. Their elastic properties enable them to function as springs. I like to call this *bounce-back ability.* Not only is God wanting to restore those dry places in your life, but He's giving you the strength to withstand future attacks and to push back against the attacks of the enemy. Claim that for your life.

Third, God spoke about the flesh. Flesh represents substance; it also provides protection for bones. God's not just interested in bandaging your old wounds; He wants to bulk you up with His Word to protect your foundation so that you can stand strong. Fourth, God goes on to speak skin onto those bones. Skin itself has three layers. Each layer serves to introduce more protection that brings stability back to this life. The attacks of the enemy cannot prosper against a woman God has spoken over. This also belongs to you. Fifth, God finishes by again calling life back into those dead situations. Today is your day to grab hold of the life of God and leave those lifeless valleys behind. I don't know what has happened in your life up to this point, but I know what you can have going forward. That is a life that reflects both the power and the love that God has for you.

You may be thinking, *Well, these blessings were for the children of Israel, not me.* The Bible says, "Know ye therefore that they which are of faith, the same are the children of Abraham" (Gal. 3:7). Jesus died and rose again for you so that the blessings of the Jews could come upon you (see Gal. 3:13). The same spirit that raised Christ from the dead lives in you, and if you allow Him, He will continue attacking those dead areas in your life and bringing them back to life *again* and *again* and *again* (see Rom. 8:11). God indeed has committed His *again* to you, but you also have an *again* that you must do.

> *Why are you in despair, O my soul? And why are you restless and disturbed within me? Hope in God and wait expectantly for Him, for I shall again praise Him, the help of my [sad] countenance and my God* (Psalm 43:5 AMP).

When things look their worst and you feel like you will not survive, put your hope back in God, not the circumstance. Trust in His love for you and *again* praise Him, even in the midst of your pain. Your praise is your faith in action.

Nothing is sweeter to the ears of God than when His child chooses to rest in Him while the storms are raging. It's not always easy, but it is worth it.

When my husband and I began trying for our family, we were diagnosed with infertility. I thought the day we sat in that doctor's office, hearing his opinions about our pregnancy chances, would be the toughest day of my life, but I was wrong. Our first attempt at pregnancy resulted in the loss of twin boys. I had never wanted anything more in my life, and I had already begun arranging my life for those beautiful boys. The pain and guilt were more than anything I had ever experienced. I blamed myself, because I felt that my body had betrayed my babies. I never thought I would smile again. I didn't want to. To be honest, I felt like being happy again would be saying that it was okay that I lost them, and it wasn't. It still isn't.

The grief began to take over my life. I sat and cried in the same spot every day. It was like quicksand, drawing me in deeper and deeper. I didn't want to do anything. I didn't want to go anywhere. And I started to resent my husband because he wasn't depressed like I was. I remember him telling me that I needed to try and move forward, to which I yelled back in disgust, "Excuse me if I'm not over it like you! Clearly, my love for my boys was more than yours!" I cringe now just writing that, let alone the fact that I said that to him. He too was grieving, but he had decided not to let it swallow him. But I was dry and brittle, and I didn't know where to begin to even want to live again. Several weeks later, my father, whom I worked for, decided it was time for me to preach again. I was furious. I could barely even stomach speaking to the Lord to ask for a message. It was strange. I knew God was not to blame for my loss, yet I was angry that He had allowed it to happen. *What on earth am I supposed to say to someone else over a pulpit,* I wondered.

That's when the Lord put this message of *again* into my heart. Even when I was dry, confused, and angry, He brought me to Ezekiel 37 to show me that He wanted me to hope again. I ministered that message the next day. I cried several times through the message. It was very hard to get through. But as I exhorted the people about God's great love and restorative power, He started attaching tendons and flesh back to my bones. I wish I could say that overnight I broke out of that prison of despair, but this was the start of that recovery. Less than a year later, I became pregnant with my son, Lucas. I was happy, but cautious. About two months in, the doctor put me on bed rest because the baby had begun to tear away from my uterus. I thought to myself, *Not again.*

Fear certainly tried to come upon me like never before, but something was different this time. When God breathed life back into my withered bones, a renewed strength came along with it. I was like those bones with new tendons, flesh, and skin. I had an extra bounce that I didn't have before. It's not because I deserved it; as I've already shared, I was mad at God and didn't want to get better. But when I allowed that word to water my hopelessness, He brought me out stronger. If you let Him, He will do the same for you. I have a beautiful boy sleeping in the room next to me even as I write this chapter. The memory of my boys is still painful, but the joy that my son brings me is abundant.

It's been several years since my painful loss, and I no longer think of it daily, but you know what does speak to me each day? The life of Lucas. You've already read about the many attacks that have come against him in his short life, but the faithfulness of God has shown through *again* and *again*. Give your pain to God, and let Him into the darkest parts of your soul. You may not see how anything could ever be okay *again*, but trust Him. Give Him your broken pieces and watch Him restore them *again*.

PURPOSED

At times in our lives, we feel as if darkness has won and the grief will never end. Storms do come. In those moments, I love to reflect on Matthew 14:6–14, where Jesus showed us how to break the back of depression and grief. At that time, Jesus was dealing with great sadness as He had just learned that His cousin, John the Baptist, had been brutally killed by King Herod. It was bad enough that he had been murdered, but the details surrounding it made it even more painful. Because of her hatred for John, a woman convinced her daughter to dance seductively for the king so that the king would have John killed. Anytime we lose a loved one, it's difficult to make sense of it, but to accept that he died because a lust-filled king received a lap dance from a strange woman's daughter would have been difficult for anyone to swallow.

I can only imagine what Jesus was feeling, but I find so much to learn in how He chose to respond:

When Jesus heard of it, he departed thence by ship into a desert place apart: and when the people had heard thereof, they followed him on foot out of the cities. And Jesus went forth, and saw a great multitude, and was moved with compassion toward them, and he healed their sick (Matthew 14:13–14).

It is understandable that Jesus got into a boat and headed to a deserted place to collect His thoughts and regain His strength in the presence of the Lord. He got into the boat, but what got Him out of the boat? It's the same thing that will pull you out of your boat of grief and despair—*purpose!* Jesus saw the people—their sickness, their needs, and the oppression that weighed upon them as they followed Him. And He healed them. He could have been annoyed by their lack of respect. They weren't allowing Him to grieve in peace. Instead, His heart moved with compassion. He remembered *why* He was there: to set the captives free, to bring deliverance and hope to the lost, and to heal the sick and brokenhearted. His purpose would not allow Him to stay locked up in grief and sorrow.

Listen, majestically created woman of God—the Lord has a purpose for your life as well. It's time to get up and be about it. Power and provision are resident in your purpose. Don't allow yourself or others to belittle it. No matter how small it may seem, it is important. Leave the forbidden fruit and all the drama behind. You have too much purpose out in front of you to waste your time with those things. The devil fights you so hard because he wants to diminish your capacity and paralyze you, but he is powerless against a woman who knows who she is in Christ.

God has not changed His mind about you. He is keeping your heart beating for a reason. I believe we are living in the last days. God is not putting the scrubs in in the final quarter of the championship game. He is putting in His best players. God could have had the champions of the Bible here on earth now to help usher in His return, but He chose you. You are one of His superstars. The thief never comes for an empty house. The fact that Satan has been attacking your life should signal to you that even he sees great value in you; otherwise, he would not waste his time.

The end of your story has already been written: beauty for ashes. Jesus secured your victory with His blood, but how you walk it out is up to you. Here's a suggestion straight from my heart: Overcome self-sabotage, take control of your life, and keep your crown. These are the *Lessons from Eve*.

Conclusion

A Call to Jesus

What Jesus has done for us is so wonderful! He gave His life so that we could be free, but to receive that gift, you must open your heart and let Him in. This is the best decision you could ever make—allowing the unconditional love of God to fill your heart and your life. He wants to take all of your ashes and exchange them for beauty. Today is your day.

If you have yet to receive the precious gift of Jesus Christ, I invite you to do so today by simply praying this prayer aloud from your heart:

> *Lord Jesus, come into my heart. I believe You are the Son of God and You died and rose again just for me. I receive You now. I repent of my sins, and I choose to turn from them. Thank You for hearing*

and answering my prayer. I am loved, I am restored, I am purposed, and I am saved.

That's it! God made it so easy that even the smallest child among us can receive His life-changing gift. If you prayed that prayer, don't stop there. Find a good church home that teaches the unadulterated Word of God and get involved. Just as a newborn baby needs to be nurtured, so does your spirit. Give God the best year of your life. Stay committed to keeping His Word in front of you, and watch what He will do with your life. Congratulations, gorgeous woman of God!

About MiChelle Ferguson

MiChelle Ferguson constantly rose above criticism and unrealistic and unfair expectations in life, which inspired her to be a catalyst, spurring others on to success no matter how impossible their circumstances seem. MiChelle has made it her goal to instill a high self-esteem in others by revealing their priceless value in Christ Jesus. Today, MiChelle is the CEO of an international ministry and an award-winning flautist. A graduate of Rhema Bible Training Center, she is an author and conference speaker who travels around the world sharing what it means to have confidence, backbone, and fortitude

michelle ferguson
MINISTRIES

The vision of MiChelle Ferguson Ministries
is to take the practical and loving message
of God's word around the world so that all
will hear and have the opportunity to come
to know the one and only true Lord and
Savior Jesus Christ.

Learn more at
www.michelleferguson.org